PRODUCTIVITY FOR WRITERS

Kristina Adams

First published in 2017. This edition published in 2018.

Cover design by Kristina Adams.

ISBN: 9781980254119

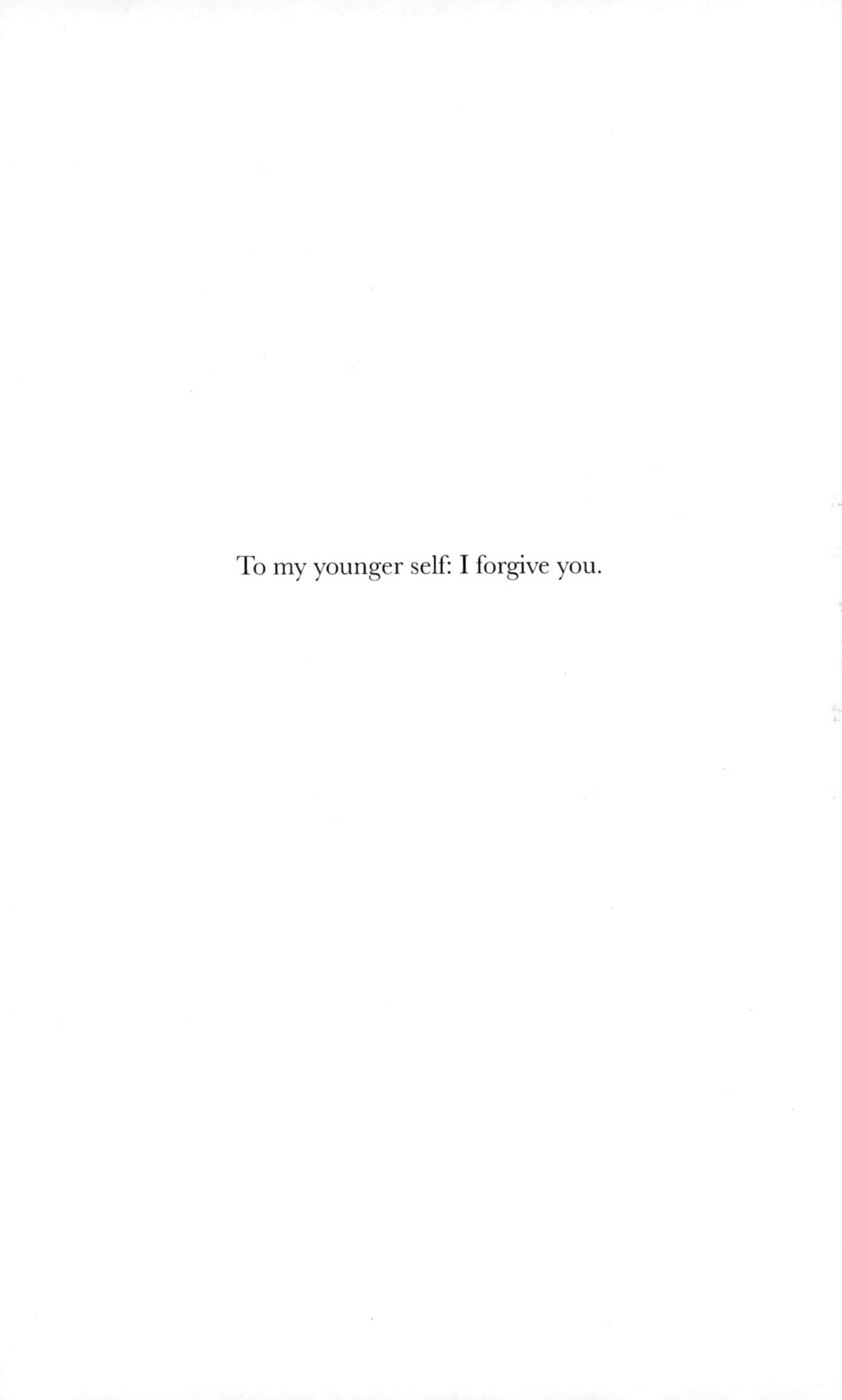

To my younger self: I forgive you.

NINETEEN YEARS IN THE MAKING

Back in 1997 I was a green-eyed, mousy-haired only child who loved to tell stories. I lived to entertain the people around me. I've done everything from play the violin to stand-up comedy in front of a crowd, but nothing has ever terrified me more than publishing a book.

Back in 1997, though, I had no idea that I was about to take my first step towards becoming a published author.

I was stood in a queue with my mum when a notebook caught my eye. It was silver and shiny and I needed it in my life. My mum bought it for me, and in doing so paved the way for me to publish my first book, *What Happens in New York*, nineteen years later.

The first story I wrote in that shiny notebook was about a stolen china teacup. I even drew pictures to go with it. I was super proud of it. So I wrote another. And another. And another. Eventually I switched to typing, but I still have that notebook as a reminder of how far I've come. And because it's shiny.

As I became a teenager, the lengths of my stories grew

and the topics I wrote about matured. I wrote less about china teacups and more about werewolves (and boys). There was some music thrown in there, too – a prerequisite of my love of poetry.

However, I didn't write for a large portion of the nineteen years between writing my first story and publishing my first novel. I never stopped thinking about my characters, but whenever I put my fingers to a keyboard, the words just wouldn't form. If the words weren't instantly perfect, or if I didn't have a great idea straight away, I'd get annoyed and stop writing. Not just for the rest of the day, but for weeks, sometimes even months.

And then my grandmother had a stroke.

It wasn't her first, but it was the first that risked doing serious damage.

If she didn't have surgery to unclog an artery, she risked having another stroke that could kill her.

My priorities changed.

I was done coasting through life.

I'd had my first taste of publication thanks to an anthology my peers and I had put together as part of my MA. I didn't want to wait until I was my grandmother's age to get published again. Or worse, die having never published a book of my own.

I wanted to make my grandmother (from hereon in referred to as 'Nan') proud.

She and Mum raised me to be career-minded. If I found a supportive partner along the way that was great, but if I didn't, I still had my career to fall back on. *That* would be my great love.

But it didn't quite turn out like that.

When I was younger, I'd always thought of 25 as the age when I'd become a successful writer (whatever one of those was – I didn't define it. This was mistake #1). It didn't happen for a long list of reasons, many of which we'll explore in this book.

Failing at a dream I'd held so close to me for so long hit me hard. I knew I hadn't really tried, though. How could I when I didn't even know where to begin?

Then I went to a workshop at Nottingham Writers' Studio on how to make a living from your writing, led by indie author and entrepreneur Joanna Penn. It inspired me, helping me to finally figure out a direction for my writing career.

In the thirteen months between that workshop and publishing my first book, I made a *lot* of mistakes. Rather than dwell on said mistakes like I used to, I see them as lessons to be learned. We'll look at some of those mistakes in this book – that way, you'll be better prepared than I was.

While I write as much as I can, I also have a full-time job as a content marketer. This means I have to juggle my job, commute, relationship, family commitments, a semblance of a social life, marketing my books, website maintenance, exercise, relaxation, and writing books, blog posts, and poetry. I don't have time for staring at a screen, willing the words to come. If I can't write, I can't pay the bills. It's that simple.

Whether you have five minutes or five hours a day to

write, we'll look at the best methods to make the most of your time. We'll also look at the main causes of writer's block, because once you know the cause of a problem, it's infinitely easier to deal with.

The tactics in this book work whether you write fiction, poetry, creative nonfiction, blogs, or anything else that involves putting words onto a page. Whether you've yet to publish or have published before but find yourself stuck in a rut on your latest project, this book can help.

Ready?

Let's go!

WHAT'S STOPPING YOU?

I was thirteen when I finished writing my first book. I paraded it around like it was a dog at Crufts. Some people were happy for me, others indifferent. I didn't care – I was proud of what I'd created. It was a young adult fantasy novel about a coven of witches, one of whom had cast a love spell. Funnily enough, it was called *The Love Spell.*

Somewhere between finishing *The Love Spell* and publishing *What Happens in New York*, I lost the self-confidence to show off my creations to those around me. I had so little confidence I seldom finished anything. I was convinced those I did share my work with only said that they enjoyed it to stroke my ego. I'd write more for them anyway – whose ego doesn't like being stroked? – but most of the time my heart wasn't in it. I was motivated by writing for other people, not for myself, and that, my friends, was mistake #2.

More than 80% of us want to write a book[1], but the majority never do.

What stops them?

And more importantly, what stops *you*?

Who's Stopping You?

Have you ever played that game where you try to work out where you and your friends will be in five, ten, or twenty years' time?

I played it once with one of my school friends. We were at university at the time, but we'd stayed close despite studying in different locations. We spoke most days; we even made each other anti-Valentine's Day cards. We were almost like Hollie and Fayth from my *What Happens in…* series.

Until she said something that Fayth would never, *ever* say to Hollie.

'Where do you think I'll be in ten years?' I asked her, eager to hear her response. We'd already discussed everyone else in our friendship circle.

She mulled it over for a couple of minutes. 'Working in a coffee shop, still trying to find the perfect idea to turn into your first book.'

Her words hit me like a punch in the face. She hadn't said it outright, but I knew what she meant: she didn't think I'd ever get published.

Hearing that one of my closest friends didn't believe in me hurt. I never asked her about it, but a part of me wishes that I had. Why did she think I'd never make it? Didn't she realise I already had an idea that I wanted to publish?

She knew about the adventures of Hollie and Fayth – by then I'd been writing about them for a couple of years – but she'd never read them. She'd never read any of my work.

It wasn't ideas I lacked, though – it was the self-confidence to share my work with people outside of my comfort zone. Comments like that didn't help.

What Happens in New York started out as a joke between my friends and I. It was my way of running away from my problems without actually running away from my problems. I posted the series online, writing/sharing chapters faster when people responded saying they wanted more. If nobody wanted to read it, why bother writing it?

I had that mentality for a long time. And that was mistake #3.

When it comes to publishing our work, it is, of course, important to think about the market. However, if you don't write for yourself first and foremost, you'll quickly get bored.

It wasn't until I started pursuing publication seriously that my mindset changed. I didn't want to show people a first draft of a half-finished story. I wanted to show them something I was proud of and that I'd worked hard on. I wanted the freedom to write scenes in whatever order I pleased, even if that meant writing the ending first.

But I couldn't do that if I shared my work as I wrote it.

The comments from others drove me to write the next chapter, maybe two. It wasn't until I started writing for myself that I realised that fuel based on other people's comments fizzles out much faster than fuel that comes from within. It's far more important to write *for ourselves* than it is for others. That way we have the chance to learn and experiment as we write. Not all of these experiments will work, but that's a good thing. Finding what doesn't work leads us closer to what does.

When one of my online friends started to come online less and less, I began to write less and less. I wasn't so interested in writing about Hollie and Fayth any more, although they never fully left me.

It took me five years to finish writing the original five-book series about Hollie and Fayth. There was also and unfinished spin-off, and an unfinished short story collection. Altogether, it was around 200,000 words. 80% of that was first drafts. For *What Happens in New York*, if I don't count the original manuscript, I still wrote 150,000 words just on that book, 92,000 of which made it into the finished manuscript. Out of the 254,000 words I wrote towards *What Happens in London*, 128,000 made it into the finished book. I also write at least four blog posts a month, all of which are around 1,000 words. On top of that, I also write one or two poems a month (sometimes more), and countless content for my day job. That's a serious increase in productivity. And all because my motivation came from within.

The Opinions of Others

Nan learned to drive a few years after she got married and had kids. Coming from a poor family with 9 siblings, she hadn't been able to afford to learn before then. Not long after she passed her driving test, she went out for a drive with her then-husband. When they got home, he said, 'You were a bit close to the kerb, weren't you?'

The next time they went for a drive together, she changed tact. She drove closer to the middle of the road. And when they got home, he said, 'Bit close to the middle of the road, weren't you?'

Mum and Nan often told me this story when I was younger to remind me of a valuable life lesson that applies not just to writing, but to every other walk of life, too: you can't please everyone. People will always pick fault out of what you do.

Let me just repeat that: *you can't please everyone.*

One last time: YOU WILL NEVER PLEASE EVERYONE.

While there are technical aspects to writing that can be taken into account and that are used to mark creative writing courses, writing itself is highly subjective. Not everyone wants to read celebrity love stories or angry poetry. Some people don't think adults should read young adult fiction (despite adults making up more than half of its audience[2]), and look down on any grown-up that does read it.

You should write a book because *you* want to write a book. If *you* don't want to write the book, the project is doomed from the start. If you don't want to write a book, you're better off spending your time doing something else, because if you don't put your all into it, you're doing yourself – and your future readers – a disservice.

The desire to receive approval from others is so heavily ingrained in us that it can be difficult to get rid of. However, if you're going to be the best writer that you can be, you need to stop seeking approval from others because you may never get it.

Not all of your friends and family will be encouraging about your decision to write. Some people will think you're wasting your time, and they'll tell you so. If you believe those people, you're stepping further away from your dreams.

A little positive reinforcement does go a long way, though. If someone you care about tells you that they love what you've written it gives your self-esteem a tremendous boost. However, you have to trust that they're not just saying that they like something to stroke your ego. Some people aren't as willing to shit all over your dreams as others are. They're just too nice to believe that sometimes you have to be cruel – *very* cruel – to be kind.

It's important to work out whose opinions are worth listening to, and whose aren't. When it comes to your writing, you should listen to the ones who can give you *constructive* feedback. This will be a combination of both good and bad, and will give you plenty of things to think about when you're done talking.

Friends and family are great, but if they're not avid readers (and I mean the kind to devour a book in a day), haven't studied literature or creative writing at degree level, and don't know how to give feedback, you need to show your work to someone with more experience. It's fine to get feedback from casual readers, but the more someone reads, the better they'll be at picking your work apart, which is really what you want. The more someone picks your writing apart, the better the end product will be.

That's where critique groups/writing workshops come in.

Critique groups very much divide the literary community. Some see them as useful while others see them as a waste of time. Personally I think it depends on the type of critique group you're a part of. I've been in bad ones where people don't understand my work, and just smile and say, 'That's good, I like that,' then move on. The ones I've found the most useful are the ones that can be the most difficult emotionally.

The important thing when finding a critique group is to find people who work in a similar way to you. You also want a group of people who challenge you. If they never challenge you, you're in the wrong critique group. Some critique groups will also help you to work out ways of fixing sections that don't work, but not everyone is comfortable with this – it varies from group to group.

Not everyone's feedback comes from a good place. People who disapprove of the path you've chosen may be unnecessarily critical. Hearing their criticism won't be fun, but you don't have to take their comments onboard. It's up to you to choose whom you listen to and whom you ignore. How you respond says much more about you than them, so if you feel yourself about to overreact, take a few seconds to think and calm down before replying.

It doesn't matter how long we've been writing or even published for, there's always room for improvement. If there's nobody around you to challenge you, this becomes more difficult. There will always be someone out there who knows something you don't and can teach you something new – you just have to look hard enough.

Toxic Friends

Think back for a moment to when you were at school. What was life like? Were you popular? A teacher's pet? An outcast?

I was somewhere between an outcast and a teacher's pet. Most of the teachers knew who I was, although I only paid attention to the classes I liked. Some of my classmates knew who I was, others didn't. For the most part, this didn't bother me. I was perfectly happy with my circle of friends.

Or was I?

We were a bunch of people who'd come together out of a mutual love of *Charmed* and a desire to survive high school. Some of us enjoyed English; others maths. Some were good at both, but tried to hide it for fear of being seen as a geek.

If someone in our circle said/did something out of line or out of character, we'd be the first ones to judge. Everyone had to fit into their neat little boxes at all times. When they didn't, it turned into *Gossip Girl*.

But I had no one else. I was too scared to move schools, and as I was the poet with an encyclopaedic knowledge of *Charmed*, no one else wanted me. I was stuck. I didn't realise just how toxic those friends were until I went to university. There I befriended people who did things for me with no ulterior motive, and would say to my face the same things they'd say behind my back. It was the first time I'd ever experienced real friendship.

The people we spent time with during our school years affected everything from how much attention we paid in lessons to whether we hung out by the takeaway and smoked or spent our lunchtimes in the library. The influence other people have on us doesn't go away just because we've finished school.

According to motivational speaker Jim Rohn, we're a product of the five people we spend the most time with[3]. If there's someone in your circle that doesn't challenge you, or inspire you, or make you feel good about yourself, why do you waste your time on them?

Make sure that the people around you encourage you to be the best that you can be and don't drag you down. If you feel that the people around you aren't the best influences, it might be time to consider moving on.

Signs of a Toxic Friend

It has to be all about them. All the time.

Whether it's in a social group down the pub or a Whatsapp group on your phone, toxic friends always have to be the centre of attention. Even if you're talking about something they know nothing about, they'll still find a way to divert the conversation back to them. It's like an extreme version of when you start talking about a dream you had, then the person you're talking to remembers a dream they had, and you never get to finish your story. Not that they were listening in the first place.

They try to tell you what to do.

Some toxic friends take things even further. Not only do they have to be in control of the conversation, they have to be in control of you, too. From dictating how you spend your time together to trying to dictate what TV shows you watch and what music you listen to, if they don't think it's cool, they'll try to stop you from doing it.

They can give criticism but can't take it.
There's nothing worse than someone who's happy to insult you but can't handle it when someone disagrees with them. We all have to learn to give and receive criticism in life. If someone can't take it, it's a sign that they're insecure in themselves and that insecurity could rub off on you, too. Feel free to stick around and try to help them, but if you've been friends for years and nothing's changed, well, you know what they say about leopards…

They're a terrible listener.
The best listeners know when to talk, and when to listen. The worst listeners interrupt you before you've even finished your first sentence. There's a difference between talking over someone because you're excited and talking over someone because you're rude, though. The people that interrupt you because they're a toxic friend do it ALL THE TIME. The people that do it because they're excited do it because they're, well, excited. The more you listen out for interruptions and people trying to take control of a conversation, the more you'll start to notice it.

Their default reaction is jealousy.

Not long after I met my partner, I had a friend who told me I shouldn't be going out with him. Said friend didn't tell me why we were a bad match, just that I was better off with someone else. He just couldn't be happy for me. Sound familiar?

Maybe you did really well in an exam, and your friend couldn't be happy for you because they'd failed, or you got an awesome job and they're not happy for you because their job sucks. Most of us can control the green-eyed monster, but not everyone can. When someone's default reaction to your good news is jealousy, it's a definite sign.

Everything is a competition.

When you say, 'I wrote 1,000 words last night,' their reaction won't be 'Cool! Nice one!' their reaction will be, 'I wrote 2,000 words last night.' Whatever you say or do, they always have to do one better than you. Everything fires up their competitive mind and they have to win.

They lean on you for emotional support, but don't always return the favour.

Sometimes toxic friendship can be more subtle. Sometimes they're not a bad person, but they dump all of their emotional baggage at your doorstep. They might return the favour, they might not, but if their emotional baggage is that heavy and they've had the same problems for years without any resolution, they need to speak to a professional. There are only so many times you can give someone the same advice.

You may feel like a bad friend, but by sapping your time and energy by asking for advice that they ignore, they're ten times worse.

You feel drained after seeing them.

The more we socialise, the happier we are[4] (even if we're introverts). But when you spend time around a toxic friend, it leaves you needing to curl up in a ball on the sofa with a DVD boxset, unable to function for the next 24 hours because they sapped you of so much energy.

Because toxic friends demand so much of our attention, it can be like entertaining a toddler – how drained you are doesn't fully hit you until they're gone. When you're an introvert, it's even worse. Being around people already drains you, but being around friends should at least make you happy. If you don't come away from hanging out with someone feeling happy, why did you hang out with them in the first place?

For someone qualify as a toxic friend they don't have to tick all the boxes. It's possible for someone to be an emotional drain without needing to be in control of what you do, just the same as it's possible for someone to try and control you without leaning on you emotionally.

How to Get Rid of a Toxic Friend

- If you only speak to them online, stop replying. You don't owe them anything – they're hurting you!
- Change your phone number.
- Be upfront. It'll likely result in an argument, but being upfront with someone who isn't good for you takes gumption and may teach them a valuable life lesson. Make sure to be tactful in your approach though!
- Drift away. When they ask to spend time with you, say you can't – you're writing. Not a lie. You SHOULD be writing.

True friendship is about balance. Real friends will do for you the same things that you'd do for them. There's nothing wrong with having friends for different occasions, like going out friends or friends you can rant with or holiday with. The important thing is that it's a mutually beneficial friendship and you're not just bringing each other down.

A true friend will be there for every part of your story, not just the good parts. True friends help to keep you going when life gets tough, and they're the first people to congratulate you when things go well. You don't even have to have lots of true friends – one or two can be more powerful than a large group. After all, if you have a huge group of friends, how many of them are you really close to?

All of this applies to relationships too, if not more so. Your partner should complement you and make you stronger, not put you down or make you feel worse about yourself.

Dealing with Negative Comments

At school I wasn't the only person who wrote poetry. But I was the only one that *openly* wrote poetry. So many of my friends were embarrassed about writing poetry because it was uncool, and they cared more about fitting in than being themselves.

There will always be people that laugh at you or look down on you for what you do whether you're a writer, refuse collector, or accountant. If you come from somewhere that reading/writing isn't popular, it can be particularly difficult to defend your time spent writing. You can even face prejudice from within the literary crowd whether you're published or not.

I've had to defend many friends that write fantasy against those that see it as a 'lesser' genre. Fantasy is hard to write – not only do you have to come up with the characters, the plot, and actually write it, but you also need to create a rich and consistent fantasy world that's either a world in itself, or that runs parallel with reality. Coming up with a plot for a crime novel is hard, but at least the world it's set in already exists. Creating a believable world from little to nothing to start you off is time-consuming and can be frustrating. Not only that, but you need a whole bunch of extra notes so that your fantastical world remains consistent.

Despite this, some of my friends that write fantasy have had their writing dismissed as 'vampire fiction' by those that decide they don't like the genre before they've even read the piece. Because vampires, zombies, werewolves, and witches are all interchangeable. And all vampire fiction is like *Twilight*.

Sigh.

Romance carries just as much stigma, if not more. There are so many crappy romance novels out there that I try not to think about it. For every Marian Keyes there's twenty poorly-written novels with two-dimensional characters and a lack of plot covered up with cringeworthy sex scenes.

Romance is cheesy. Romance is cliche. Romance is boring.

These are all things that I've heard people say. And yes, it can be but are you honestly telling me you've never said something cheesy to your partner?

Unfortunately, fiction has to be more believable than reality. This is the difficulty that all writers face.

The path you choose towards publication can also affect people's reactions to your writing. Having chosen the indie route, I have found that there are some people who are less supportive towards my work than they are of my traditionally published peers. While the stigma around indie publishing has lessened in recent years, it's most definitely still there.

Whatever you write, there will be someone that disapproves of your choices and is more than happy to let you know about it. Whether someone says you're wasting your time, or what you write is 'lesser' than something else, you can deal with those people/comments in exactly the same way.

By ignoring them.

If they're prejudiced against the genre you write in, they're not your target audience, and they're not your friends.

Your target audience won't immediately write off your novel without reading it, and your friends will support you whatever you write. So why waste your time defending your novel to someone who falls into neither category?

Not everyone will like your book, just the same as not everyone will like you. You can be the nicest person in the world, but someone will use that as a reason to dislike you. That's not your fault, and you shouldn't make it your fault. You don't need negative people like that in your life.

I was bullied a lot at school. About my looks, my work ethic, my general refusal to fit in, and of course, my writing. But my writing was the one topic where comments washed over me. I didn't care that my classmates found it weird that I wrote stories because I enjoyed it, and nobody could take that love away from me. My characters would always be there for me. The people who made fun of me never would be.

Your life is for you, and no one else.

Living your life for someone else is a half-life. It's soul-destroying.

You are the only person that has to deal with you every minute of every day, and if you don't like who you are, your life isn't going to be any fun. And life *should* be fun. And if you find writing fun, then do it. It's nobody's choice but your own.

I've seen what can happen to people who waste their lives trying to please everyone else before themselves. They get frustrated. They get bored. They get depressed. They become shells of themselves, unsure of who they really are any more. They base who they are on what other people tell them to be or do, almost like they're acting in a film of their life.

Don't be one of those people. Be who you want to be.

Take Yourself Seriously

There is one person who stops us more than anyone else, and it's someone we often forget about. It's not an acquaintance, or a friend, or even a loved one. Quite often when this person stops us, we don't even realise how much control they have.

That person is yourself.

It's so easy to fall into a trap of self-hatred and self-loathing when you spend all day inside your head. We don't see ourselves in the same way that other people do. We see distorted images of ourselves, as if we're looking through a fun-house mirror. We insist that these distorted images are real, and the more we insist on this, the harder it is to accept an alternative. We see ourselves as frauds, fakes, and imposters.

How differently I see myself compared to others never sunk in until I had a conversation with Boyfriend. We were talking about confidence, and he said that he thought I was confident. I laughed. 'No I'm not,' I said.

'Sure you are. You always talk to people.'

I didn't see talking to people I'd just met as a sign of confidence – I did it because I was uncomfortable.

I was also uncomfortable calling myself a writer, so I used to call myself an 'amateur writer' in my Twitter bio. A published author tweeted me and told me not to call myself an amateur – if I write, I am a writer. This comment had a profound affect on me. She couldn't have been more right.

Referring to yourself as an 'amateur writer', or saying 'I want to be a writer' puts you down. It's like saying you're not good enough to be a 'real' writer. What, in your mind, would be enough for you to become a 'real' writer?

If you apply for *The Great British Bake Off*, you cannot have formally studied baking or anything else food-related, or make a living from it[5]. To them, an amateur is someone who is purely self-taught. Some people feel the same about writing. If you've published a book but don't make a living from it, are you a real writer? What about if you make money from writing, but it isn't your main industry? Are you a real writer then?

If you write something, you *are* a writer. If you write poetry, you're a poet. If you write fiction, you're an author. If you write screenplays, you're a screenwriter. If you blog, you're a blogger. Putting words like 'amateur' or saying you 'want to be' something puts a barrier between you and your goal. Say that you are it, and you will become it. When we say something aloud, it acts as an affirmation. It gives us power.

You don't see entrepreneurs referring to themselves as 'wannabe entrepreneurs'. If they did that, nobody would take them or their business idea seriously. Why should you approach your writing any differently? The most successful writers are businesspeople, too. J.K.Rowling has turned *Harry Potter* into an empire with films, spin-off books and films, theme parks, merchandise, and more. James Patterson, meanwhile, doesn't even write all of his books. Yet he makes a fortune from them. They both made clever business decisions, and because of that, they both have more money than you or I could ever dream of.

I'm going to assume you're a writer, even if you don't class yourself as one. Firstly, because this book is called *Productivity for* Writers, and secondly, because you're struggling to write. I've met very few writers who don't suffer from some form of self-doubt or imposter syndrome. We're a self-deprecating bunch.

It doesn't help when you see other writers doing better than you. Seeing other writers sell more copies of their books than you or making more money than you or writing faster than you can make you wonder why you even bother.

Except that when you do that, you forget something. Everyone has a different story to tell. There are things you're better at than the people you compare yourself to. You shouldn't measure your success against other people's any more than your should compare your relationships to other people's. Everyone's stories and motivations are different. By measuring your success against other people's, you'll always come up short.

The next time someone asks you what you do, don't feel like you have to be defined by your day job. Say, 'I'm a writer'. Saying it aloud, to people you may not even know, helps to give you more confidence in being a writer.

Words like writer, author, and poet, carry authority and respect. Not as much as they used to in the Western World, but in some parts of the world you can still go to prison for writing certain types of fiction, or for challenging authority figures with your journalism. Remember that the next time you feel like you're wasting your time by writing. Whether you write pulp fiction, erotica, literary fiction, or political commentary, your writing *will* affect people. It *will* touch people. You just have to give it the chance to.

...But Not too Seriously

As with everything in life, the 'take yourself seriously' advice comes with a caveat: don't take yourself *too* seriously. It's important to be confident as a writer, but you shouldn't take yourself so seriously that you come across as arrogant. Just because you take yourself seriously, that doesn't mean that everyone will. There's no harm in taking a joke once in a while. Being so filled with pride that you think everything you create is amazing not only harms you, but also your writing and the people around you. There's no positive side to pride. Pride takes everything too seriously. Pride stifles you creatively.

So while you take yourself seriously as a writer, remember that that's not all you are. You're also a family member, a friend, a partner, a pet owner. You're so many things to so many people – a writer is just part of the complicated equation that makes you who you are.

The Monsters in Your Head

We all have our inner demons. Some come in the form of anxiety. Others alcoholism. Some even parental issues. What your demons are, only you know. But all demons come after us at some point. And fighting those demons is the hardest thing you'll ever do.

I've struggled with inner demons since I was a teenager, and they're something I've learned to live with only recently. Not long ago, I hated myself. I hated myself so much that I couldn't function. I was broken, physically and mentally exhausted simply from existing. I had all the time in the world to write. And it terrified me. I was so crippled by my fears that instead of embracing the opportunity, I wasted it: I wrote less than I ever had. I imploded.

It wasn't until a friend suggested that I do an MA that I started to see a glimmer of hope. My MA was one of the best things that ever happened to me. Thanks to that course, I'm part of a talented and friendly writing community and have friends all over the world.

That doesn't mean the demons went away, though. The further into the course we got, the more pressure I put on myself. I had to do well. I HAD to. I put so much pressure on myself that the long-term stress took its toll. I developed a plethora of physical and mental health issues. Zombies had more energy than me. The day I handed my dissertation in, I went out for lunch with a friend. I finished eating then had the overwhelming urge to vomit. I went home and was ill for a week.

I vowed never to put myself through that again, but demons that powerful are difficult to vanquish. I put a colossal amount of pressure on myself while working on *What Happens in New York*, and it left me physically and mentally drained for months after the launch – worse than after my dissertation hand-in. I hadn't learned a thing.

I stopped having the energy to socialise. I wanted to crawl into a hole with my Richelle Mead books and stay there. But I couldn't. I had too many other things to do. I had fans who wanted to know what happened next to Hollie and Fayth and I didn't want to let them down; I was excited to write the next part of the story; I also had to carry on with my day job and daily life.

When you redirect your anxiety into something productive or positive, it helps you to deal with it and can even boost your performance[6]. That's why I continued writing. And you know what I found? It did help. I looked forwards to my daily writing sessions and they helped to keep me going when I felt low.

I used to write less when things got bad, almost as if I was punishing myself. But what was the point? What did punishing myself achieve? It made me feel worse, and it made it more difficult for me to recover from what had happened. I will never go back to running away from writing again.

Writing helps us get out our pent-up emotions, process things we can't get our heads around, and escape to a different world when life is tough. It's a coping mechanism, just the same as exercise or alcohol or baking. Maybe you turn to other methods too. But if you want to finish that novel, writing should be your main source of therapy. Nobody else can make it your priority.

Striving for Perfection

Some people see perfection as a badge of honour; a cross to bear that they just have to carry the burden of. They use it as their biggest weakness in a job interview, as if wanting everything you create to be flawless is even possible. But it's not. Perfection is not your friend: it's a snake that wants to bite you. And that bite could be lethal to your creativity.

For some of us, our desire to create something perfect can stop us from even starting the creative process. We want every word to be world-changing from the moment we put it onto the page. If it isn't, it's not worth writing at all. This is a dangerous fixed mindset, and one that it's worth avoiding at all costs if you want any form of writing career. Writers with this mindset are often the ones that fit into the tortured artist cliche but have very little to show for all their melancholy. Writers who are tortured do not create because they're tortured, nor are they tortured because they create. Sylvia Plath and Dylan Thomas were incredibly talented writers who both died tragically. They weren't great writers because they were tormented, though. Their writing would've been just as powerful if they hadn't been depressed. They may have written about different things, but talent like that doesn't go away just because your mindset changes.

Agile software developers don't chase perfection because they know it doesn't exist. They aim to fail fast and create the best product they can at that time. Failing fast is such an important part of their philosophy that FailCon is an annual conference dedicated to all things failure.

Developers also know that 'done is better than perfect'. Software development is expensive – businesses can't afford to wait until a product is perfect to release it. They release the basic features first, then continue to add in new features and updates as the company grows. In theory, this could go on forever.

While you can't publish your writing then make drastic changes to it later on, you can write an infinite number of words before you show anyone a thing. The more you write, the more you'll get a feel for your voice, and the more you publish, the more your confidence will grow.

There's a lot of self-publishing advice out there that suggests you should publish your books as fast as possible. While I can understand this from a marketing point of view, if you want to build a long-term writing career, your fans will be far more loyal to you if you take your time writing your books – it's easy to tell when something has been rushed.

Perfectionism gives you a false sense of security. It tricks you into thinking you'll be protected from criticism because your creation is faultless. Except that just because you think something is perfect, that doesn't mean everyone else will agree. As we've already discussed, there will always be someone who picks fault out of what you do. That's why it's so important to think about what you want first and foremost.

What makes something perfect varies from person to person. Striving for perfection cripples us. It stops us from moving on because we obsess over the minutiae.

Don't dwell on why your piece isn't perfect. Fix what you can. Aim to write the best thing that you can at that moment. Your best at 17 will be infinitely different to your best at 27 or 57 or 107. Always keep the bigger picture in mind. Publishing your first piece of writing isn't the end of your writing journey; it's the first step.

There are no signs, neon or otherwise, to tell you when something is ready to share with the world. You will never be 100% happy with what you've written. Sometimes you just have to publish it and see what happens. And you know what? It's scary. But the more you do it, the easier it gets.

Even when we love something, there will be elements that we dislike. Many people love writing stories but don't enjoy the editing or the pitching or the marketing that goes along with it. If you just want to write and aren't interested in publication, then that's what you should do. If you want to get your writing published, you have to ask yourself if the good outweighs the bad. If it doesn't, it may be time to consider a different creative pursuit.

That being said, you shouldn't feel the need to finish every piece that you write. How we feel about a project that we're working on can make a huge difference to how easy or hard it is to write. Don't feel compelled to finish something (unless you're being paid for it, in which case, sorry, but you've just got to get on with things). We can outgrow our writing projects just like we outgrow our children's clothes. That doesn't mean working on it was a waste of time. Take the lessons that you can from your abandoned project and use them for your next. That way, each project you work on will be better than the last.

Permanently putting a project in the drawer can be hard. If you feel you've outgrown it or you don't enjoy working on it any more, though, you have to ask yourself why you still spend time on it. Are you getting paid (or will you when it's finished)? Will it attract the attention of agents and publishers? Will your target audience enjoy it? Even if you think it might attract the attention of agents or publishers, or your audience will enjoy it, remember that they're not dumb: a writer's passion for their project comes across in their writing. They will know if you don't love what you're writing about. They'll know if you're writing for the sake of writing.

Write what feels right to you. Don't feel obligated to finish projects you don't like (once again, unless you're getting paid to write). The time you waste on those projects could be better spent on projects that you do enjoy.

And remember: not a word you write is wasted. They're all part of your writing journey, and they all help to make you a better writer.

It's time to forgive yourself and accept that neither you nor your writing will ever be perfect. Life is a journey. The most successful entrepreneurs never strive to be perfect – they strive to be better. From Bill Gates to Beyonce, they know that there is always more that they can do to up their game and make their business/brand better. You should treat your writing exactly the same way.

Signs of Stress and Burnout

Think of your energy levels like a battery. Certain things recharge that battery, while others drain it. You may find dealing with people draining, while alone time recharges you. You may find that some days writing helps you to recharge, while on other days it drains you. It can depend on what stage of the writing process you're at, or what's going on in your life outside of your writing.

Just like when you let your phone battery get close to 0%, the lower your battery levels get, the longer it takes to recharge.

Physical symptoms:

- Fatigue
- Insomnia
- Shortness of breath (and exacerbated asthma if you have/had it)
- Palpitations
- Chest pain
- Random aches and pains with no discernible cause
- Weakened immune system (making you more likely to develop colds or viruses)
- Loss of appetite
- Stomach pain and digestive problems such as cramps, indigestion, heartburn, irritable bowel syndrome, constipation, and diarrhoea
- Headaches
- Dizziness/lightheadedness

- Fainting
- Hair loss
- Weak and brittle nails
- Skin problems, from acne to eczema and everything in between

Psychological symptoms:

- Memory problems
- Anxiety
- Depression
- Irritability
- Anger
- Loss of interest in things you used to enjoy

When you're burned out, there really is only one thing to do: rest. It's a lot harder to give your all to something if you've only got 10% battery remaining.

Whatever helps you to recharge, do it. For me, it's trashy TV and true crime documentaries. You know I'm ill when I binge watch the latter.

Even if you're an introvert, there may be people who help you to recharge just by their presence. Spend time with them (or if they're too far away, chat to them on Skype or FaceTime). Talk to them about what's going on inside your head and why you're so drained. If you can't, don't be afraid to sit in silence – with real friends, there's no need to constantly fill the void. They won't love you any less for it.

Most importantly, get hugs. Hugs from loved ones and

even our pets make us feel better[7]. That's why animal therapy is used in some hospitals and nursing homes. Animals listen and love us without judgement, and there's something very special about that.

Don't let your battery get so low that it leads to the problems listed above. Take the time that you need to recharge. If you're already burnt out – or think you might be getting close – speak to your doctor. There could be other factors at play that drain your battery more quickly than others, such as a vitamin D deficiency (which can cause/ exacerbate depression), or fibromyalgia (which can leave you constantly drained).

While there isn't a cure for everything that drains us, there are ways to deal with them. The more of these things that we have, the easier it is to recharge when we're drained.

What drains you?

Make a list of everything you do daily, every few days, and every week. On the next page, split it down the middle. On one side write down tasks that drain you, and on the other side write down things that help you to recharge. If you're unsure, think about how you feel during and after certain activities. What leaves you smiling? What makes you want to reach for your duvet? Some things may have a more significant effect than others.

When you've finished, think about how you spend your day. Do you spend more time on activities that drain your battery, or on ones that recharge it? Is there anything you could do to distribute them more evenly throughout your day?

You can't avoid every task that drains you, but breaking up your day so that you don't spend all day on draining activities keeps your battery levels steady and helps you to avoid burning out.

Why You Can't Always Think Like a Writer

Everyone's minds work differently. Our minds often deceive us into making the wrong choices, especially when self-doubt creeps in. Asking ourselves what our loved ones would do – particularly those that are wired differently – can make a huge difference.

You're a writer. Your brain works in strange ways. The chances are you're a sensitive soul, and that's great. It makes it easier for your readers to connect to the stories you tell. But it doesn't necessarily help with your productivity levels. The slightest set back – be it a negative reaction from someone or the monsters in your head wreaking havoc – can stop you from writing altogether. And in doing that, it becomes a longer and more winding path towards reaching your goals.

But I've developed a way of dealing with those emotions: I ask myself what two of my closest allies would do. Nan and Boyfriend are the two strongest people I know. Nan has been through two bouts of cancer, two strokes, and a heart attack. To call her resilient would be an understatement.

Boyfriend, meanwhile, is the yin to my yang: he tackles things with logic first, emotions second. He sees every mistake as a lesson to be learned.

So when I hit a roadblock, I speak to them. Nan is an incredible listener, and if she doesn't know how to help she'll say so. But that doesn't matter. Sometimes just talking about my challenges helps me to work through them.

If Boyfriend has issues, he speaks to someone whose opinion he values or who has a different skillset to his. He isn't afraid to ask for help, but until he needs it or the project he's working on is ready, he won't show it to outsiders.

If I can't speak to them and the challenge is imminent, I put myself into their shoes in the same way that I do with my characters. How would they feel? What would they do?

Nan and Boyfriend take what lessons they can from their mistakes, then carry on. They won't say something is easy if they don't feel it is, but they won't complain either. Complaining doesn't change the problem, it just means it takes longer to find a solution.

Talking to outside influences – particularly non-writers – helps to give a sense of perspective when things go wrong. At the end of the day, it's just a a few words on a page. There are scarier things than writing. Like getting an endoscopy. Or quadruple bypass surgery. Or spiders.

Who inspires you?

Who's a big influence on you? It could be a parent, a sibling, even a celebrity. Next time you have a decision to make, or are reacting to a particular situation, take a moment. Ask yourself how that person would react. There's a chance that you're overreacting to said situation. Or under-reacting. Or that there's a better, easier way to deal with what's in front of you.

Who do you spend your time with? Who's the most influential in your life? Write down each of their names, then write down their most significant traits. If their negative traits outweigh their positive ones (refer back to the section on toxic friends if you're unsure), it's time to rethink how you spend your time.

Out of the positive traits, think about which you could adopt or need to work on. If you're not sure how to achieve a particular trait, speak to that person – you're already close to them, so it's highly unlikely they'll say no!

Everyone has their own way of dealing with things. No way is better than any other, just different. The more alternative points of view you can factor in, the more solutions you have for solving a problem. Alternative viewpoints also help us to stay open-minded and bounce back more quickly from failure.

Location, Location, Location

In June 2016, Boyfriend and I bought our first house. I wrote more in those first few weeks than I had in years.

Why?

Because I was somewhere new.

The flat we'd lived in before, while in a good, central location, was filled with negative connotations for me. Of waking up at three o'clock in the afternoon and wasting the rest of the day watching *White Collar*. Of sitting in candlelight, banging my keyboard because I couldn't focus. Of trying too hard but at the same time not trying hard enough. I got more writing done when I was away from the flat, but I was too anxious to go out regularly on my own. So instead, I hardly wrote at all.

I wrote the majority of *What Happens in New York* in the living room of our new house, sat on the sofa, with no TV or internet access. After I published it, we converted the box room into a writing room so that I could hide away and write with as few distractions as possible. The more things you have around you to distract you, the harder it is to focus.

If you don't spend a lot of time at home, it can be the best place to relax. It's often where we feel most comfortable and able to unwind. Now that I spend more time away from home, I definitely find it's the best place for me to switch off and get some writing done.

However, when you spend a lot of time at home and you're used to watching TV, cooking, listening to the radio, browsing the internet, doing chores, and the menagerie of other things you do at home, focusing on something can be difficult. If this is you, you're probably better off working somewhere else. When you're somewhere quiet, such as a library, you feel obligated to be quiet and to concentrate because everyone around you is doing the same. The atmosphere can be contagious.

Most cafes and pubs are happy for you to spend some time there to get some writing done, too, if you don't mind a little background noise. Places that offer free newspapers or free Wi-Fi are the ones most likely to be happy for you to stick around.

If you're self-employed or fortunate enough to already write for a living, you could also try co-working spaces. Many offer open days or daily rates so that you can check them out before signing up for a membership. Co-working spaces are great for people who spend a lot of time on their own but prefer the company of others. However, if you're a talkative type make sure you don't speak to your fellow co-workers unless they're happy to be disturbed.

You don't have to have your own writing room or pay for a co-working space to have somewhere to write, though. Your writing space can be anything from a beanbag in the corner of the lounge to your car. It should be wherever you're most relaxed and free from distractions. If you haven't found a place like that yet, think about which places you feel most comfortable. Is it at home? Is it your local pub or cafe? Your local park? Try out each place, and see how much work you get done. Try it a few times, if you want. You don't have to commit to anywhere.

One place I would advise avoiding is your bedroom. The more time you spend in your bedroom not sleeping, the harder it is to get to sleep[8]. This means if you spend long periods of time writing, editing, watching TV, or scrolling through your phone while lying in bed, your brain will find it harder to switch off when it's time for sleep. When your brain associates your bed/bedroom with sleep, it finds it easier to switch off when you're in that room.

If you really can't avoid writing in your bedroom, at least

try to avoid doing it in your bed. Have half your room for work (your desk area), and the other half for sleeping. That way, your brain will still associate bed with bedtime, and nothing else.

Your environment matters

There are many factors that can help you to work out how suitable a place is for you to write in. Things like lighting, noise levels, and even what kind of chair you sit in can make huge differences to how much you achieve.

Natural light will always be better for you[9], but if you can't get that, aim for lights with a white hue not a yellow one, as they're closer to natural light.

Make sure you're comfortable in whatever chair you sit in, as you'll be there for a while. If you have coccyx problems like many people in my family do, invest in a decent chair and/or a coccyx cushion, which has a hole for your coccyx to take the pressure off it. These cushions can make a huge difference if the chair you sit in doesn't offer much support, but if you've got a decent quality chair this shouldn't be as much of a problem.

A decent chair will give you the ability to adjust the height so that your knees are parallel to your desk. Your arms should naturally rest at the height of the desk, and your hands and wrists should lie flat against the keyboard. Unless you don't know where all of the keys on your keyboard are, there's no need for the keyboard itself to be at an angle. Ergonomic keyboards that further take the strain off your wrist also exist, although many of them look like something from a sci-fi film.

Your monitor, meanwhile, should be directly in front of you so that you sit perfectly straight. The more twisted you are when you sit at your desk, the worse it is for your body. The top of your monitor should be at eye level, which further helps you to sit up straight. An external mouse and keyboard, and a laptop stand, can help if you use a laptop.

Noise preferences vary from person to person. When I'm out, I like ambient noise. As soon as I can understand another person's conversation, it's too loud for me. Some locations will be quiet during some times of the day and noisy during others, so you may want to keep this in mind, especially if you plan to work somewhere like a cafe or a park, which are likely to be busier at lunchtimes or after school/work.

Even something as simple as the temperature of the room in which you work can affect how much work you get done. You have full control over the environment in which you write, so take advantage. Try as many different locations as you can until you find something that works. If you feel, after a few weeks, that you're no longer as productive in a particular location as you used to be, try somewhere else. You may find you need to work in a new location every time. From your back garden to your local pub, there's an almost never-ending list of places you can sit and write.

Over to You

Make a list of everything that stops you from writing. Be honest with yourself or this exercise won't work. It can be anything from the voices of self-doubt, to the mounting laundry pile, to work, family, whatever.

It doesn't matter how long your list is. Nobody's judging you. Really think about what's stopping you from writing. Be brutally, painfully honest with yourself.

You don't have to show your list to anyone – you can even destroy it when you're done reading this book (but not before – you'll need it later on).

Now rank everything on your list from 1-10. 10 being it stops you regularly and is non-negotiable, 1 being it occasionally stops you and there are ways you can work around it. If you want to do one column for how often things stop you and another for if they're negotiable, that's fine.

How many things are on that list? What's ranked the highest?

Here's a look at mine, as an example:

- Work and commute - 8
- Chores and gardening - 6
- Family - 5
- Relationship - 3
- Self-doubt - 8
- Anxiety - 7

While the top thing that stops me from working on my books is my full-time job, I enjoy what I do and don't earn enough from my books to pay the bills. My commute takes about an hour to an hour and a half out of my day, though, so I need to be careful I don't waste that time. We'll look at ways to write around a commute and full-time job later.

Gardening, on the other hand, isn't something I enjoy. There's also two of us in the house. If we work together on the garden and stay on top of it, mowing the lawns and de-weeding weekly/fortnightly instead of when we can be bothered, it takes half an hour here or there, rather than longer because it's been neglected. The same applies to chores – the more people within a household that chip in, the faster they get done. The faster they're done, the more time everyone has to spend on what matters to them.

Things like chores and gardening can offer much-needed brain breaks between writing sessions. They give you time to think about issues away from the screen/notepad, while still being productive (and getting some exercise!). You could even use the opportunity to catch up with your favourite podcast or listen to an audiobook. Short periods spent washing up or ironing add up, so never think that it's a waste to listen to a book or podcast at the same time. You'll get through them even faster if you listen to them on 1.5x or 2x speed. It may sound weird at first, but you get used to it after a while.

Another thing that can take up my time is my family. While they would never stop me from doing anything, sometimes their health problems mean that they need my help more often. It's occasions like this when my writing takes a step back. Supportive friends and family make a huge difference to your writing, your productivity levels, and your mood. Partners are no exception to this. Whether you've been in a relationship five days, five years, or fifty years, spending time together is important. Boyfriend and I regularly go to the cinema together – especially if there's a new Marvel film out – eat dinner in front of the TV – especially if there's a new Louis Theroux documentary out – and go shopping together. If it's been a while since we've done something together, we'll schedule some time together so that we have something to look forwards to. Scheduling time with loved ones may feel like a chore, but it ensures that no matter how busy you are, they don't get neglected. Friends and family are important, and they can be great sources of inspiration and encouragement, too. You can also use your time with them to celebrate different milestones.

Out of all of the obstacles that I face when it comes to my writing, the biggest ones come from within. My biggest regret used to be the black hole I fell into after finishing my BA. But now, whenever I start to beat myself up over what I've done, I remind myself of how much I've changed since then, and what that period in my life taught me. I don't want to waste my life feeling sorry for myself; hating myself; not getting out of bed. I want to spend my life working towards what I want, not running away from it.

However, I refused to believe that I was good at writing, and at the end of each session – while I was often happen that I'd written *something* – I was seldom happy with what I'd created. So I'd abandoned my work in progress and not write again for a while. I'd completely missed the point: you don't get better at something without practise. Much like you'll get better at weightlifting if you lift weights regularly, you'll get better at writing if you write regularly.

And, mostly importantly, you can do as many drafts as you like before you show your piece to your dog, let alone your friends, family, editor, agent, publisher, etc. First drafts don't have to be perfect. We all fell over the first time we walked. It was new to us. How could we not? The first draft of a project is us learning to walk again. It's a constant learning process, and that's a good thing. Life would be boring if there was nothing left to learn.

Now, go back to your list.

What's *really* important?

WHY DO YOU WRITE?

When I first committed to publishing *What Happens in New York*, very few people believed that I'd stick it out. I didn't blame them or hold it against them. I still don't. I'd committed to so many projects and gotten bored when things got tough that I wouldn't have believed me either. But something was different this time.

Almost losing one of the strongest people I knew reminded me of how short life is, and how we need to take advantage of every moment.

Nan has always been the wisest person I know, and by far the best listener, too. It's something I've apparently inherited. I've had people I've only spoken to once or twice tell me their darkest secrets in the hopes of getting some advice. Giving advice is something that's always come naturally to me, and while I haven't always thought this to be a good thing, I've always loved helping people.

It's the thought of helping people get over the same hurdles that I struggle with that keeps me blogging, and that motivated me to finish this book. I went through so much in the year it took me to write and publish *What Happens in New York* that I'll be Nan's age before I realise all of it and share everything I learned.

Working on *What Happens in New York* also helped me to realise what I want to achieve with my writing: I want to offer people an escape, and I want to inspire people. I want to inspire my readers to write more, write better, stop procrastinating, chase their dreams, spend time with their loved ones, and look after themselves. These are themes that run throughout my fiction, poetry, nonfiction, and blog. They're themes that are important to me, and that have even rubbed off on those around me.

The question is, why do you write?

What's Your End Goal?

So you want to be a writer. But *what do you want to write?*

Think of all the projects you've worked on in the past, are working on right now, and plan to work on in the future. Which means the most to you? Which will you feel the proudest at having published? What would you love to see in the hands of your parents/children/significant other?

That is the project you should focus on.

That should be your end goal.

When you have to turn your friends down for coffee, or miss an episode of your favourite show, you need to know why you're doing it. Whether your end goal is to finish a writing project, self-publish it, or get it published traditionally, you need to want it desperately. This gives you the power to keep going even when you don't want to. And, no matter what your project is, there *will* be times when you don't want to work on it. When that period is varies from project to project and person to person, but you will face that hurdle at least once during the writing process (maybe even more than once). At this point, you may fall prey to procrastination. You may desperately feel the need to clean the guttering or do some other asinine chore you've put off for the last five years. Suddenly the urge will become uncontrollable and you'll do everything *but* write.

And that's when you need your end goal the most. That's when you need a deadline. That's when you need to visualise a copy of your book in your parent/partner/child's hands, or picture your article published in your favourite newspaper.

The only way you'll get past your mental hurdle is by forcing yourself to keep going. Nobody else can force you to do it. You are the only one that can jump over it. But if your will to jump over it isn't strong enough, you'll find every reason not to, and then some. Your end goal *must* be important to you, or you'll never reach it.

What if your end goal is further away, though? What if it isn't just to get one piece published, but to build a long, prolific writing career? Well, the rules still apply. Start small and work your way up. The only way you can become a prolific writer is by writing one word at a time. When your writing goal is so long term, it can be particularly difficult to stay motivated. However, it can also help to keep you focused when one of your pieces doesn't perform as well as you'd hoped. When you aim for a long, prolific writing career, a couple of pieces failing to reach your expectations can easily be cancelled out by the ones that exceed them.

How Do You Define Success?

I mentioned earlier that one of the mistakes I made was not defining what being a successful writer meant to me. Some days I wanted to be an author, others a poet or a screenwriter. Some days I just wanted to get paid to write anything. But would I have defined any of these things as success?

For most, success is publishing a book. Just the one. Some writers that I've met – even highly educated ones – believe that publishing their first book will be a cure-all. They think they can take early retirement and pay off their mortgage from their book advance. Sadly, this is becoming less and less likely. The average author in the UK earns just £12,500 a year[1]. That's £2,000 less than minimum wage if you work full-time. When you factor in how long writing, editing, publishing, and marketing a book takes, it works out at even less.

While you can make money from writing, it's highly unlikely this will happen from the first book that you publish. It may not happen from the second, either. The average book sells just 250 copies in the US per year. Many are only published for a few years, then they get discontinued if sales aren't enough for the publisher to justify another print run.

The more books you write and publish, the bigger your platform and audience will become, and the greater your chances of earning a living from your books. Whenever you publish a new book, your backlist gets a boost, too, because your latest book appears in the new releases section in bookshops. If it's part of a series and a reader likes the looks of it, the chances are that they'll read the rest of the series, too. Keep this in mind when you're only selling a book a month and wondering why you even bothered.

The pay for poetry isn't great either. Many successful poets these days (for instance, Kate Tempest or Rupi Kaur), built their platforms on social media or through music, and receive higher sales because of their already established fanbase.

Journalism pay varies from publication to publication, so do your research before you pitch somewhere. Local newspapers can pay as little as £40 for your hard work; even big newspapers may only pay £100 a piece. However, if you get one piece published a day, that's not such a bad payday after all.

There's more money in screenwriting, but just because a studio buys your screenplay, that doesn't mean that it will get made. Scripts that do get turned into films often turn into the director's vision, not the writer's, and other people may be hired to significantly rewrite your script, too. Proceed with caution if you cannot emotionally detach yourself from your writing. (That being said, this is a skill every writer needs to learn one day.) For a prime example of what can happen to your script once a studio has acquired it, compare the film and TV versions of *Buffy the Vampire Slayer*. The TV show was

Joss Whedon's vision. The film version was about as far away from it as you can get.

There are other ways to make money from writing – competitions, freelance journalism, editing – but they're seldom well-paid. If you're looking for something that pays well, try channeling your creativity into marketing or software development instead.

Achieving our dreams takes a level of work many of us aren't willing to put in. It means spending every spare moment on it, then finding more spare moments when doing everything from waiting in a queue to going to the toilet. There will be times when you're working the equivalent of two jobs to pay the bills and publish your books, and it won't always be fun.

If you write for the love of the craft, none of this will matter to you. This is the best way to stay motivated. Writers that give up when things get difficult don't love writing as much as they claim to. They like the idea of it, but not the hard work that goes into achieving it. Writing will only ever be a hobby to them. It's like a friends with benefits situation – they love the writing, but not the hard work that comes along with it.

Other writers define success as critical acclaim. There are many, *many* literary awards out there. Some hold more weight than others. Many only accept traditionally published books and poetry, but there are exceptions, particularly as the stigma around self-publishing continues to change.

Critical acclaim is another way of receiving approval

from others. Not receiving it can leave us disheartened, but you don't need other people to tell you that you're allowed to write. It's your life – you can do with it whatever you like.

Some people define success as qualifications in creative writing or English literature. While these are great to have, many of us don't follow the career path that our degrees lay out for us. Out of the thirty people I went to university with, just three of us are published. Most of my peers found the process overwhelming or fell into the corporate world and haven't found their way out yet. If you've fallen into this trap, it's not too late! There's no reason you can't have corporate and creative success.

Rejection is Your Frenemy

Rejection is the one toxic friend you can't and shouldn't get rid of. The more rejections you get, the closer you get to acceptance.

There isn't a single published writer out there who hasn't been rejected at least once. In fact, I think you'd struggle to find a writer who's *only* been rejected once. Even Stephen King had short stories rejected when he first started out[2]. Harry Potter was rejected by numerous publishers, and J.K.Rowling had some pretty harshly-worded rejection letters for her Cormoran Strike novels, too[3].

Some authors get to the point where their name alone is enough to attract the attention of a publisher. To get to that point, though, you have to go through what feels like endless rejections. Many writers don't get past this point. They don't have the gumption or the tenacity or the drive to keep going.

When it comes to rejection, there are two types of people in the world. Those of us that can handle it, and those of us that can't. The people that can handle it are the ones that brush it off and move on. They're the Hilary Clintons of the world. Those of us that can't handle it treat each rejection as personal. We assume that it means our work isn't good enough and we must therefore stop trying.

But that's the wrong mindset to have. And it *is* possible to change mindsets.

When I first upped my PR game I really struggled to get coverage. I reached out to places intermittently, dreading the inevitable rejection email – or worse, being completely ignored.

After working with several sales/PR experts and reading Janet Murray's *Your Press Release is Breaking My Heart*, I finally found the gumption to keep pitching until something stuck.

And then I got accepted by The Huffington Post.

This was a huge achievement for me. While I'd been blogging for years, I'd always struggled to get my writing placed elsewhere. Getting my writing published in The Huffington Post meant that I finally had my foot in the door. And once your foot is through the door, it's a whole lot easier to get the rest of your body into the room.

Unfortunately, the door will be slammed shut on your foot many, *many* times before you make your way into the room. The first few times it will hurt and will feel like they're trying to cut the circulation off to your foot (or in this case, your creativity). If you keep going, it will feel like you've stubbed your toe – it'll sting like hell for a few minutes, then everything will return to normal and you can carry on. If you keep going after that, you'll get to a point where rejections don't hurt any more.

Sometimes you don't hear back because someone missed your email – in a busy inbox it's easily done. Sometimes you get rejected because it's not what a magazine/blog/publisher is looking for right now, they've published something similar recently, or your piece is great but doesn't fit their audience. It's never as simple as your writing being good or bad – it's almost always about the right time and place with just a little bit of luck.

Before you hit submit, do your research. Know who the best person to contact at a publication or agency is and email or call them directly. Make sure you know what they're looking for and be confident that your writing is a good fit for their audience. Don't just contact an agent because they're an agent. Doing so is a waste of both their time and yours.

Even after spending hours researching and tailoring your writing style to somewhere, you may still get rejected. You may not even get told why, but after a while, rejection becomes just another part of the process. Because it is. Not everyone will like your creations. The most important thing is that you like it, and that you enjoy the creative process.

If you find the prospect of marketing and publishing your work daunting, don't worry. It gets easier with time. The short-term stress and heartache is worth it for the joy of sharing your work with the world. And there will be people out there that want to read it, I promise. But *you* have to find *them*.

Rejection is as important to the writing and publication process as drafting, redrafting, and editing. While it's never fun to receive a rejection (although there are some writers who frame rejection letters or keep rejection emails), they help to build resilience and a thicker skin for later on in your writing career. Your list of rejections may always outnumber your list of acceptances, but so long as you keep persevering and get your work out there, none of that matters. It only takes one acceptance to change your luck.

Over to You

I want you to really think and be honest with yourself for a moment. Sit quietly, and answer the following question: why do you write?

It doesn't have to be *War and Peace*. It could be a paragraph, or even just a few words. Be sure that you don't write because you feel like you should, or that you're missing out on something if you don't.

If you can't think of anything, don't worry. It took me years to realise what the common themes and messages behind my writing were. You might be the same. That's fine. But you won't figure out what those themes and messages are unless you write profusely.

Next, answer this: what do you want to achieve with your writing? Do you want to make a living from it? Do you want to see your name in print? Do you want to increase awareness about a particular cause/issue? Do you want to share a personal story? Take your time with this. The answer may not be immediate.

When you're first starting out, sometimes the only reason you can come up with is enjoyment. That's perfectly OK. However, there's a big difference between liking and loving something. You liked your teenage crush. You love the person that you marry.

Liking something and loving something are worlds apart. Writing should be so high up on your list of loves that you can never get bored of it. You may get pissed off with it, but you'll never grow tired of it. No matter what you're doing, you'll always want to go back to your writing: everything you do is a potential source of inspiration. If you only like writing, studying it will put you off. If you love writing, you'll do anything you can to keep that love affair alive whether you've been writing five months or fifty years.

Loving writing means that no matter what happens in your life, your motivation will always come from within. That is the most powerful force that can drive you forwards.

You may find your motivations change over time. It's only natural given how much we can change as we get older.

Now that you have your answers, you can start to create an action plan. What can you focus on first that will push you closer towards your goal? Is it writing more? Doing more research into the areas you write in? Attending courses to learn about new types of writing? It could even be going out there and living your life instead of hiding behind your computer screen.

If you're still unsure about why you write, don't worry. The more words you write, the more you'll start to notice themes and discover what topics you're really passionate about.

Sometimes to achieve our dreams we have to do things – or hear things – that we don't like. This is all part of the journey. Just as with a relationship there will always be things that annoy us about our partner, there will always be things we dislike about writing. So long as the pros still outweigh the cons for you, then stick to it, because you can and will get there.

HOW MUCH TIME DO YOU REALLY HAVE?

There's a huge difference between being busy and being productive. Being busy means your time is occupied. Being productive means you're making the most of the time that you have and you're working towards a goal.

Technically speaking, you're busy if you're scrolling through Facebook. But are you being productive? Nope.

We've all had days where we spend more time perusing the internet than getting things done. We look like we're doing something, but at the end of the day, we've achieved nothing.

When you really want to achieve something, you have to sacrifice other things to be able to do it. The more you want to do something, the more you'll be willing to sacrifice to get there. There will always be things you can cut out, cut back on, or compromise on in order to reach your goals.

A while ago, there was a story that made the rounds on the internet. It was about a guy who walked three miles in the blistering Texan heat to work at a fast food restaurant everyday[1]. All because he wanted a car. Walking saved him money, and his job gave him money towards a car. He wanted a car badly enough that he was willing to walk six miles a day to do a job many of us would turn our noses up at even if it was just down the road.

When we want something badly enough, we're willing to put the work in to get it. From making sacrifices to changing our mindsets, there are lots of things we can do to push ourselves closer towards our goals. Whether you want to write and publish a novel or get published in a popular newspaper, if you want it badly enough, you'll put the work in to get what you want.

The question is, how badly do you want it?

Create a Routine

It's great when you feel inspired, but if you're serious about a writing career, you have to write when you're uninspired, too. You can't sit around and wait for inspiration to strike. It may never come. The more you sit around waiting for 'the muse' to magically appear, the less likely she or he is to show up. It isn't like that episode of *Charmed* where muses follow people around and inspire them, and when they're not with us we can't write speeches or put words together to form a poem (or in their case, a spell). In real life, the muse isn't some magical, ethereal creature. The real muse is in your head, and it's a creature of habit. Much like when you exercise your muscles become stronger, your ability to come up with ideas when you're not in the mood to write or not feeling particularly creative gets better the more you do it.

Routines can seem drab, boring, and grown-up. But they work. If you decide to write when you get home from work – and actually stick to it – eventually your brain will *want* to write when you get home from work. Eventually, not writing when you get home from work will feel odd.

Having structure to our lives and something to work towards helps us to keep going when the monsters in our heads try to take over[2]. Life can feel meaningless when you're battling depression, but that end goal can give you a focus that's loud enough to drown out the monsters. It also helps to free your mind of the confusion and fog that anxiety can create, and gives you a clear path to follow.

Routines can also prevent you from procrastinating as you know that there are things you *must* get done.

Sticking to them at first can be difficult, but having a reason to keep going and someone to hold you accountable helps to keep you focused. It also helps if you're doing something that you enjoy.

The amount of time that it takes to build a routine depends on its complexity[3]. It also depends on how much you want to create your routine. If you don't really want to do something but feel like you should, you're far less likely to achieve it.

Your first step could be to get up slightly earlier and use that time to write. For the first week you could aim for five minutes of writing, then ten minutes for week two, and gradually increase how long you write for as you get into your routine. Once you reach the end of your time frame, stop.

Actively deciding you'll do something is a big step – the first step towards forming your routine.

If you can't stick to a particular time frame because of family commitments or shift work, pick an achievable word count instead. This allows you to be flexible about when you write, but ensures you still have a writing goal for that day.

Every so often, there will be days when you don't hit your word count. It could be because family are visiting, you're on holiday, or you're ill. While writing should be your priority, there will be times when other things require your attention. Don't punish yourself for that. Be aware of what barriers stopped you from writing and think about what you could do differently. If you couldn't write because you were ill, focus on getting better instead.

Breaking a routine is much easier than fixing/creating one, so when you do take a break from your routine, be mindful of that. Going to the gym gets a lot easier once you get used to it. When you stop, it becomes intimidating again. You come up with a million different things you need to do instead. A writing routine can feel the same. That's why it's so important to be consistent and make sure whatever you want to achieve in your writing routine is attainable. The more attainable it is, the more likely you are to stick to it. Not only that, but every time you reach (and surpass) your target, you'll feel a great sense of triumph.

Family Matters

When you have children, time really is precious. *Especially* if they're young. While your time and energy is devoted to them, it's still important for you to have time for yourself. I spoke to some writers with children about how they fit writing in, and most said that they write while their child is at childcare or nursery. Or, if they're really desperate, when their child is asleep.

Speak to those around you and see who can help with childcare. Explain to them your situation and ask them if they'll help you out by looking after your child(ren) for set periods each week. This gives you time to yourself to focus on your writing, and your child(ren) someone new to play with for a few hours. (We both know how boring parents can be.)

When you first start working on your project, the people around you may not understand. The demand on your time may be high, particularly if you're the person responsible for the everyday running of the household. That's why it's important to ask for help and support from others. Make everyone in your household – or that's a regular visitor – aware of what you want to achieve. They may not understand initially, but the more dedication you show to what you're doing, the sooner they'll come around.

To save everyone in your household time, get everyone to chip in with the chores. The more people that are involved, the faster they can get done and the more time everyone has to spend on their hobbies and interests. If other people in your household aren't used to helping with chores, start by giving them short and easy tasks. Explain why you'd like their help (because you'd like more time to write), and, to make things such as chores more fun/appealing, try turning them into a game. Set a time limit and offer an extra couple of minutes of TV time for each item they put away before the timer is up, for example. Even if you don't have kids, you could still use gamification for tasks you don't enjoy, writing-related or not.

Many people are stopped from chasing their dreams by family life, but by continuing to chase your dreams no matter what age you are or how many children you have, you set a positive example.

If you write for children and you have a child around the same age as your target audience, you could use them as your very first beta reader. Who better to test out your writing on, or to hold you accountable? It's a great way to spend time together and gives you both something to look forwards to after a long day.

You could even take it one step further and include them in the creative process – get their opinion on character names, plot points, or run dialogue past them. It's a lot harder to think like a target audience when you're no longer a part of it. Younger audiences are one of the fastest-changing, particularly with technological advances, so having someone within that target audience you can run ideas past can be really useful. They could even act as a source of inspiration.

Make notes whenever you have an idea – even if it's just a quick trigger word – and plan as much as you can before your writing sessions. The more you can do before your writing session, the more productive your session will be.

Unfortunately, due to the unpredictability of being a parent, this doesn't always work. Sometimes you just have to sit in front of your computer/notepad when you have a few minutes to spare, and write. Even if you hate what you write, at least you've tried. And the more you try, the easier it becomes to summon ideas when you have a few minutes to spare.

Life as a Carer

How do you find the time to write when your life is dedicated to caring for someone else?

In all honesty, you'll probably struggle more than most people. Finding time isn't impossible, but it's tough. There are groups out there for carers, and for people with most conditions. If you can find somewhere that can look after the person you look after for a few hours each week, that gives you some time to yourself. You could also ask other people the person you care for is comfortable with to look after them for a few hours once or twice a week. If there isn't anyone, see if there's someone you could introduce. Most towns and cities have volunteer centres, so if you don't know someone you may be able to find a good samaritan willing to help out.

As I mentioned in the parenting chapter, there are always people willing to help out if you ask. Asking isn't always easy, but you'll be a better carer if you take some time out for yourself once in a while.

What to do When You Bite Off More Than You Can Chew

It wasn't until I was in the midst of *What Happens in New York* that I realised I may have bitten off more than I could chew. Not only did I have a book to write, but I also had to edit and proofread said book, format it, design the print and ebook covers, market it, and organise the launch event. When you're already working full-time and you have five or so hours a night to do all of that – as well as other projects, chores, relaxation, exercise, and maintaining some sort of social life – it leaves you very short on time. But, as it was the first book I'd ever published, I didn't realise how long these things took when I set the publication date. I thought the writing would be the hardest part. Oh, how wrong I was.

If you find yourself with more to do than you can handle, there's only one solution: prioritising. Not just in your writing, but in your life, too.

It can be difficult to drown out the white noise when there's a lot going on, but President Eisenhower had a technique for this. He created a table that compromised of four boxes, now often referred to as the Eisenhower Box or Matrix[4]. Items on the top left were marked as urgent and important; top right were marked as important but not urgent; bottom left items were urgent but not important, and on the bottom right they were neither urgent nor important. Tasks marked as important and urgent he'd do straight away; important but not urgent tasks he'd do later; urgent but not important tasks he'd delegate to someone else, and tasks that were neither important nor urgent he'd eliminate.

Even though Eisenhower was president in the 1960s, his technique is still popular now. Why? Because it works.

The next time you don't know what to focus on, put your tasks into this matrix. How much time do you spend on unimportant and non-urgent tasks? How many tasks could you delegate or cut out altogether? You'll be surprised how little is as important as you think it is when you start organising your life in this way.

Family commitments are important, but supportive family members will pick up the slack if you ask. That's what they're there for! Friends can be a great help too, and you can play to their strengths. Know someone who works in marketing? Bribe them with coffee to help you with your social media! Got a friend who's a graphic designer? Take them out to dinner in exchange for a book cover! The more you can delegate tasks that you need to do but that take time away from writing, the more time you have to write!

If you can afford it, you could even hire a virtual assistant, or VA. VAs can do everything from sending emails to booking your hair appointment – whatever it is that takes up your time that someone else could do instead. There are sites out there where people will do good jobs for a very low rate. However, when it comes to services, you will always get what you pay for.

If the idea of getting someone else to do your dirty work sounds abhorrent, ask yourself this: is your 'yes' mentality burning you out? Do you say yes to tasks you don't want to do just to make other people happy? People will try to take advantage of this. As horrible as it may make you feel, there's nothing wrong with saying no.

Learning to say no when you're a 'yes' person is tough. You want to please people, I get it. But, as I mentioned earlier in the book: *you can't please everyone*. The longer you spend trying to please other people, the harder it is to work out what *you* want. The harder it is to work out what you want, the more likely you are to become depressed and burned out. And then you're no good to anyone.

When it comes to saying no, instead of saying that you can't do something, say that you don't do something. When you say that you can't do something, it's a restriction. It implies that you would if circumstances were different. Saying that you don't acts as a self-affirmation[5]. So instead of saying, 'I can't miss my writing sessions,' say, 'I don't miss my writing sessions'. The language we use reflects who we are, and changing that language makes a huge difference to how we think and feel over time.

Multitasking is NOT Your Friend

They say that women are better at multitasking. Who this 'they' is, I'm not sure, but they shouldn't be encouraging women – or men – to multitask.

Multitasking isn't good for productivity. It's terrible for it[6].

The more tasks you do at once, the more your focus is split. When you're constantly flitting between writing, IMing, tweeting, having a conversation, researching something, and watching TV, your brain can't give anything its full attention. Because of this, you're more likely to get confused and make simple mistakes.

Doing more than one thing at a time is tempting, I know. I used to be a compulsive multitasker. Now that I try to focus on one task as much as possible, I'm consciously aware of how much multitasking affects my productivity. I write far more when I'm listening to music than when I'm watching TV. Listening to classical music has been proven to help make you more productive[7]. There's no such links to watching TV, and I doubt they'll ever come. How can you write and watch TV at the same time? You're paying attention to two conversations, two sets of visual cues, two stories…it just doesn't work.

However, if you're doing something monotonous or that doesn't conflict with what you're doing – such as listening to a podcast while doing the ironing – it doesn't have such a detrimental effect. A little background noise such as a podcast, some music, or an audiobook can help make the time go much faster when you're doing something repetitive or tedious.

How many projects are you working on?

You're also multitasking when you work on several writing projects at the same time. While it doesn't matter so much when you write short content, working on several longer projects at once makes it confusing and means you'll take longer to finish things. It's just as bad as reading several books at once.

Imagine you're reading three books at the same time. One's fantasy, one's romance, one's a biography. Each night you read a chapter from each. Because you're only reading a chapter at a time, it takes you longer to finish them all. Not only that, but there's the chance of confusing the plots, characters, and stories. You're going to enjoy a book a whole lot more, and be more immersed/invested in its world, if you read one book at a time. You'll be hypnotised by the mythology of the fantasy book; drawn into the sexual tension of the romance; enticed by the wisdom of the biography. But your feelings won't be as intense if you're not giving those books your full attention.

The same applies to your writing. When you write a fantasy novel and a romance novel at the same time, you're going to confuse the plot and characters, especially if your time is already limited. It also means that it will take you longer to finish those projects, and therefore longer to reach your goals. Working on both projects at the same time means that you won't be as immersed in the worlds, and therefore, your readers won't be either. When you split your focus, you lose some of the attachment that's crucial to create a world your readers can connect with. You just can't be immersed in three worlds (reality included) at once. It's too confusing. Do. *Not.* Do. It.

The longer you immerse yourself in a particular world, the easier it is to drown out the other ones you've considered crafting. A couple of years ago, I started working on a romance/crime novel. I really enjoy working on it, but it's had to take a backseat until I get further into the *What Happens in…* novels. I have a plan for that series, and I know where most of the characters are headed. I don't have the same direction for the romance/crime novels.

I think about the characters sometimes, and come up with ideas for them. When I do, I write them down somewhere safe so that I don't forget anything and I'm not trying to cram everything into my head. I'll either leave a trigger word or phrase in my Notes app, or I'll write out the passage in full, ready for when I return to that project.

At present, I have twelve books planned (including this one). If I were to split my time between these projects, I wouldn't get very far. There'd also be an even bigger gap between each of my books being published.

So I have to prioritise.

Putting one project above all else allows us to finish projects and improve faster. If you never finish a work in progress, you'll never get better at the whole process. For example, if you always stop writing a poem halfway through, you may have killer titles and opening lines, but your endings won't be as strong.

This process is even more important for books – we've all read a book where the opening is strong but the ending falls flat. Whether it's at the end of a book or at the end of a series, there's nothing worse than emotionally investing yourself in a book only to be disappointed with how the characters' lives end up.

The only way to avoid giving this feeling to your readers in your own work is to see projects through to the end and not abandon them when things get difficult or you're drawn to a different project because you're bored of your current one. Finishing every book that you read is another way of improving your endings. The more you read, the more you'll learn what works and what doesn't, and what kinds of things have been overdone and therefore need to be avoided.

Managing the Day Job

Having a full-time job can make finding time to write difficult. With forty hour work weeks and the average commute in the UK verging on two hours a day[8], that's a lot of time dedicated to the day job. If you happen to be one of those people with a two hour commute, though, it doesn't have to go to waste.

You can achieve a *lot* in two hours. You could write your character biographies. Plan your novel/blog post/article. Write it, even. Public transport is great for things like this, so take advantage. You wouldn't be the first writer to work on something during their daily commute, and you definitely won't be the last.

If you're on a crowded train/tram/bus and can't move, there are still options. Put some headphones in and listen to a podcast or audiobook; catch up on blogs; read an ebook on your phone; do some research for your next project; proofread your manuscript or latest blog post; you could even write a first draft on your phone. There's nothing worse than wasting your commute staring out of the window like a zombie.

You have fewer options if you drive to work, but you can still make the most of this time. You could listen to podcasts and audiobooks in the car, or to music that inspires you.

Lunchtimes, meanwhile, don't just have to be about eating. Lunchtimes are useful for getting away from your desk, both physically and mentally. Use your lunchtime to exercise or write, depending on what facilities are available to you. Whether you get half an hour or an hour, you can use the time to yourself to plan, write, edit, market, and do whatever else it is you need to do for your writing.

Most of the time I use my lunch break to go for a walk around town. One of my friends also works in town, so we meet up once a week to catch up. She's also a writer, so if I have any issues I need to work through she's more than happy to help. Seeing one of my friends at lunchtime helps me to relax, puts me in a good mood (especially if I've had a bad start to the day), and can even inspire my writing.

Your day job and your writing can work together if you manage your time well. Your job can be a good break from your writing, and your writing can help you to relax after a long day. Having all day to write sounds like a great idea, but it can make it even more difficult to stay motivated.

Why Boredom is a Luxury

There's a huge difference between boredom and relaxation. Some people find sitting with their eyes closed focusing on their breathing boring. Others find it relaxing. What is relaxing for you may not be relaxing for other people, and vice versa. Relaxation is important for us to recharge not only our creativity, but our bodies and minds in general. The more relaxed we are, the easier it is to focus.

Boredom, on the other hand, is a luxury.

If you are bored, you are wasting your day – maybe even part of your life – away.

If you have a goal you want to achieve and you've not yet achieved it, how can you possibly be bored? Why are you not spending every spare moment you have working on it? Every minute you spend being bored is a minute wasted. It's a minute where you could've achieved something and become one step closer to your goal. Boredom is a luxury. If you live a fulfilled life where you're actively seeking to improve and reach your goals, you should never feel bored.

When you have too much time on your hands because you're too young to work, you're unemployed, you're retired, or you simply don't need to work, it's difficult to stay motivated. You are the unlucky ones.

When I was younger, I would often whinge to Mum and Nan that I was bored. I'd end up watching TV or doing website stuff to pass the time. The website stuff proved to be beneficial for my future career. You could argue that as I wanted to be a screenwriter as a teenager, watching TV was also productive, but I wasn't *actively* watching it. I took nothing from it; I didn't analyse it. It was just there. I consumed it passively and obsessively.

Since starting my full-time job, I don't have time to be bored. When I'm not at work I'm commuting, eating, socialising, sleeping, writing, or doing something else related to my writing. All of my time is taken up. I cannot remember the last time I was bored. And you know what?

I like it.

I don't want to be bored. I don't want to waste my life not knowing what to do with it.

When you don't have any sort of routine, it's difficult to create one for your writing. Being self-disciplined is tough because you can do what you want whenever you want. Having no sort of daily routine also makes it easy to put off simple tasks. You have all the time in the world. Why does it matter if you don't do something right now?

Because the more you put off, the less you'll achieve.

The less you achieve, the more you'll regret.

Start off by deciding what you want to achieve. Even if you really do have all day to yourself, don't start off by aiming to write all day if you don't write anything most days. Start off with several short writing sessions throughout the day. As the days go on, build this is up so that you can write more and more. You could also try something such as the pomodoro technique[9], where you spend twenty five minutes on a task, then take a five minute break. After four cycles, you take a 15-20 minute break, then start again. There are lots of similar methods out there, so give a few a go and see how you get on with them.

Procrastinating Your Life Away

We've all fallen prey to procrastination at some point. The trouble is, once you fall into the habit of procrastination, it's difficult to get out of it. You find yourself more and more attracted to doing pointless tasks, like watching videos online or scrolling through social media. You know it's a waste of time, but you just can't stop yourself.

One of my favourite ways to procrastinate used to be playing mobile games. I spent hours playing them. They helped with my anxiety more than anything else (until I started binge reading), so whenever I felt anxious, I'd start playing. In hindsight, I wish I'd channelled that nervous energy into writing or reading or even exercising, but at the time, it was the easiest option. When I committed to writing, I forced myself to stop playing these games, reminding myself of just how much time I'd wasted on them. When I needed to clear my head, instead of playing a game, I'd open my laptop or a note on my phone and write something, or pick up a book. Eventually, this became my default. I feel much more productive doing this, and also a lot calmer.

When I wasn't feeling anxious, I used to come up with other excuses not to write. I wasn't in the mood. I wanted to watch a new episode of *Castle*. I had to talk to someone about something.

It was all bullshit.

In reality, I was just afraid. Of completing a particular task, of triggering a particular emotion, sometimes of even of *starting* a particular task. By putting off said tasks, I was just making my anxiety worse. I was delaying the inevitable, meaning that by the time I had no choice but to do something, my anxiety was through the roof. If I'd done it sooner, my anxiety wouldn't have been so overwhelming.

You may also feel that your work will never be good enough, so why start?

The answer to all of these things is simple: until you start, you'll never finish. Not finishing your projects means you won't learn or grow, and you won't become closer to your goals. Instead, you'll stagnate. You'll still be doing the same thing in five years' time that you are now.

Don't become that person.

Over to You

Refer back to the list you made for What's Stopping You? about your priorities. How do you *really* spend your time? How much time do you waste watching television? Scrolling through Facebook? Watching cat videos?

Remember to be honest with yourself here. You won't get anywhere if you don't.

Before I started work on *What Happens in New York*, this is what my list outside of work looked like:

- Watching television
- Scrolling through Facebook/Twitter/Instagram
- Baking
- Visiting Mum and Nan

- Going for coffee with friends
- Sleeping in late

Before I committed to working on *What Happens in New York*, I watched a *lot* of television shows. I'd spend several hours a night catching up on my favourite shows, as well as some I didn't really care about. If it was a quiet time of the year, I'd rewatch some of my old favourites. I dread to think how much time I've frittered away watching shows over and over. I even re-watched episodes that I hated. Why? I'm not going to like season eight of *Charmed* any more the second, third, or fourth times around.

I still watch new episodes of my favourite shows, but I use them as a reward, or a pick-me-up. I don't *have* to watch them the night they air. I record everything I'm interested in watching, then binge watch them when I'm ill or in need of some down time. A few years ago it would've been unheard of for me to go a day without watching TV, but these days I can go over a week and not even miss it.

There are many popular TV shows out there that it feels like *everyone* watches. Just because everyone watches them, that doesn't mean you have to, though. Your friends may love *The Walking Dead*, but you may loathe it. If so, why are you watching it? Real friends won't ditch you just because you don't watch the same shows that they do, and if you really are great friends, there'll be plenty of other things you can talk about instead.

The second biggest time suck for me was social media. I'd

fallen into the trap of scrolling through social media aimlessly, reading articles or looking up people I hadn't spoken to in years. But really, why? The more time we spend on social media, the less happy we are[10]. Not only that, but people generally only post the happy stuff and things they can brag about. This gives the illusion that their lives are better than they actually are, which makes you feel worse. Why do that to yourself?

Social media is important for marketing, but if you spend all your time on it, it sucks away precious time like a leech sucks out blood. Instead of frittering hours away each day, schedule posts to your accounts using tools such as Buffer or HootSuite, or set aside a few minutes each day to catch up on things. If you really can't stay away, the Tools to Try chapter offers some browser add-ons which may help.

Habits are hard to break. As I mentioned earlier, I finally broke my bad habits when we moved house. I made a conscious decision to change as a person when we moved, and I did. I spent every evening writing until bedtime. I managed 50,000 words by the end of July, having only started the first draft in June, right in the middle of moving.

Boyfriend and I both value our work. He therefore understands when I need to write, just as I understand when he has programming to do. We make sure to spend time together regularly, though. Spending time with friends and family is important for our mental health. But so is hanging out with the right people. Before you arrange to meet someone, ask yourself why you're meeting them. Do you actually care about them? Are they just going to talk about themselves the whole time? Are they interesting to talk to? Are they a toxic friend? Don't waste your time on people who are more interested in themselves than you, or who just drag you down. The time you waste on these kinds of people is better spent elsewhere.

Sleeping in late is another luxury many of us don't need. Sleep is important for us to recharge, but the later we get up, the less we get done. Many of the world's most successful entrepreneurs and businesspeople are early-risers[11]. Some of them get up as early as four or five o'clock in the morning. This may sound insane, but these people get shit done better than some of us could ever dream of. Most of them also start their day with exercise. There's a reason for this. Exercise wakes us up and readies us for the day ahead. It also helps to relieve stress, and strengthens our minds and bodies.

If you prefer to write at nighttime, ask yourself why. For me, it was the peace and quiet that comes along with it. Writing also helped me to switch off after a long day. You can still get peace and quiet first thing in the morning, though. Some places are even quieter in the morning than they are at night. If you really can't avoid writing at night, set yourself a cut off time so that you still have a consistent sleeping pattern.

Look back at the list you made at the start of this exercise. Which of those things do you *really* need to do? What do you get out of each of them? Ditch anything that you do to kill time or that worsens your mood. Necessary evils – like chores – you can schedule in, get other members of the household to help with, and even turn into games to make them more fun. Things that you don't learn anything from or that aren't writing-related, you can cut back on and use as a reward or way to relax.

MAKING THE MOST OF EVERY MINUTE

I used to loathe plotting my novels because I felt like it sapped the creativity from the writing process, and I hated planning out my time because I wanted to live my life freely and spontaneously (read 'freely' and 'spontaneously' like 'freely!' and 'spontaneously!' for the full effect).

And you know what?

I was an idiot.

When I was a student or unemployed, I had too much time on my hands so I didn't prioritise things because I didn't feel that I needed to. When I got a full-time job, I realised that being organised actually does help you to achieve things no matter how much time you have.

With only a few hours to spare each evening, I could spend that time perusing the internet or watching TV, or I could write several thousand words and be one step closer to my goal. Thinking about this every time I felt disheartened or uninspired kept me focused.

Before you dismiss any of the tactics in this chapter, make sure that you fully commit to them for at least a week. If you've done a half-ass plan of your book, then no, you won't find it useful, nor will you find free writing useful if you're also scrolling through Facebook and chatting on the phone at the same time. The only way to find out if something is really for you is to try it with an open mind. There are plenty of people out there willing to put you into a box. Don't restrict yourself by saying that you can't, don't, or won't do something before you've even tried.

Write EVERYTHING Down

When your mind is swimming with ideas and things you need to do, how can you possibly concentrate on anything?

The solution is simple. It's something you've already done several times since you started reading this book: make a list.

The more things you get out of your head and down on paper, the less crowded your mind is, and the easier it is to stay focused. Keep a list of general, day-to-day things, like getting the car washed or watering the plants, then keep a separate one for your writing.

Bullet journaling[1] – which is kind of like a to-do list on steroids – is another tool you could try. Each list is given a topic and a page number so that you can easily refer back to it, and items on the list are broken down into tasks, events, and notes. I use a watered-down version for both work and personal organisation, and I find that I achieve so much more than I used to.

While I use a pseudo-bullet journal for day-to-day tasks, my long-term goals are written down separately. I keep them specific and add deadlines to as many as possible. Deadlines mean that we *have* to do something. If we don't, there could be consequences. The consequences aren't as severe for self-imposed deadlines as they are for work-related deadlines, but you'll still feel disappointed if you don't reach them – especially if other people are aware of your deadline. (We'll look into accountability buddies in more depth later on.)

However, there's a huge difference between working to a deadline and leaving everything until the last minute. When you leave your writing until the last minute, you have less chance to mull over your ideas, edit things that don't work, and make your work in progress the best it can be before you share it with the outside world.

The further away your deadline is, the more tempting it is to put things off until later. I've seen people do this with dissertations then wonder why they didn't do as well as they'd wanted to. Rather than leave everything until the last minute, get your first draft done as far away from your deadline as you can. That way, you have months to work on your writing and make your project the best it can be. There's nothing wrong with finishing something ahead of schedule. The sooner you finish something, the faster you'll learn and can move on to your next project. Just because it feels like you have an infinite amount of time to do something, that doesn't mean that you do. Life can be unpredictable. It pays to be prepared.

If you don't get a task done by the deadline, ask yourself how important it *really* is. If it's not that important, why did you want to spend your time on it in the first place? Focus on what's *really* important, and discard the rest (refer back to the Eisenhower Box if you're unsure).

You'll never achieve *everything* that you have to do. Once you accept this, you're a) a lot less hard on yourself and b) more willing to focus on the tasks that really are important.

If you're worried you'll forget something, set a reminder. Setting reminders is particularly useful if you prefer to write to time constraints, or if you've only just started your writing routine.

Plan Ahead. Way Ahead.

When I start a new project, the first things I write are the beginning and the end. If I don't know where a book ends, I'm less likely to finish it as I don't know what the characters are running towards. The sooner I have the ending worked out, the easier I find it to finish the first draft.

This has *always* been true for my writing, even pieces that will never be published. I used to have a terrible habit of coming up with characters, writing a great opening, then having no idea what to do next. These stories quickly fizzled out. Anyone who'd read what I'd already written would never discover what happened next because I didn't know either, and I didn't care enough about the characters to find out.

What Happens in New York was the first novel I ever fully planned. Before that, I'd only attempted a plan on one other occasion – for my MA dissertation. However, it was a half-ass one that I created just to satisfy my dissertation tutor. (Sorry, if you're reading this! I've since learned that you were right!)

Not fully planning out the novella I wrote for my dissertation is where I feel I most went wrong with the whole process. Had I planned it out in more detail, I would've been able to pick up on the plot holes/weak points faster and would've had more time to fix them.

It wasn't until I started working on *What Happens in New York* that the importance of planning truly hit me. The further into the novel I got, the harder I found it to remember what was going on where. I needed certain things to happen on certain days. I could only keep track of that, and make sure that it happened, if I wrote down the plot. There are far too many characters in the *What Happens in…* universe for me to get away with not planning. Not planning risks neglecting characters and missing crucial points in the story.

There are writers out there who don't believe in planning. I'm not here to convert those people. However, I find it very hard to believe that they don't have anything tucked away in their heads about where they want their story to end up. That, my friend, is still planning. The only difference is that they haven't written it down.

Not writing your plot down is fine if your life is care-free and revolves around writing, but if you're short on time and need to clear your head, writing down what you want to happen and when means you can't forget anything. There are many topics in this book that never would've been covered had I not written them down when the ideas came to me. We've all come up with a great idea only to forget it before we get chance to write it down. When you write something down as soon as the idea comes to you, there's less chance of this happening. There's also be fewer things cluttering your mind, making it easier to concentrate on what's in front of you.

Make sure to keep your planning and writing time separate. They're two very different disciplines – if you're training yourself to free write, you'll find it harder for your brain to learn how to do it if you spend one day free writing, the next planning, then back to free writing, etc. If you only have half an hour a day to work on your project, spend fifteen minutes of that planning and the next fifteen free writing.

Of course, you don't have to have everything planned out when you start writing. As long as you have a couple of points worked out, you have somewhere to take your characters. You can always figure out the rest as you go.

If you're not sure where to start when it comes to plotting your novel or screenplay, *Save the Cat*[2] is a good place to start. While the book is aimed at screenwriters, many of the rules apply to any plot-driven form of writing. Your story doesn't have to follow a conventional structure, but until you know the rules, you can't break them. Many stories that aren't planned out still follow similar structures.

Even if you do have everything planned out, there's no reason things can't change as your characters and story grow. Plans should be flexible, not concrete. Your characters should still be capable of surprising you. Having a rigid plan for your story can be very restrictive, and have the opposite effect of what you're trying to achieve. Alternatively, not having enough of a plan can cause your characters and story to be all over the place. Finding a balance between the two will make your writing process both easier and faster.

If you're working on a series, plan out as much as possible. The further ahead you plan, the less work you'll have to do the further into your series you get. J.K.Rowling wrote the ending to *Deathly Hallows* not long after she finished writing *The Philosopher's Stone*[3]. That may seem obsessive, but it's not a bad idea. Planning so far ahead allows you to foreshadow future events. Readers will then notice new things and read new meanings into events each time they read it.

When it comes to poetry, things get a little more complicated. Whether or not you find planning out your poems useful depends on the kinds of poems that you write. Most of my poems, for example, are micropoems. If I planned them out I'd likely spend more time planning them than actually writing them. There's no way that would be a good use of my time.

However, if you write narrative poems, want to follow a structure you don't usually write, or you want to convey a particular message, planning out your poem can help you to adhere to the story, structure, or message that you want without going off on a tangent. Having a clear plan can make the editing process much easier because you can pinpoint exactly where you went wrong.

Out of every form of writing, nonfiction is the one that most benefits from planning. Planning out your nonfiction means that you know which areas you need to cover, where to add in subheadings, and you can create a structure that's easy for readers to follow, making them more likely to keep reading. The average attention span is now just 8 seconds[4], so having a clear, concise style to your nonfiction is imperative.

Break it Down

A few years ago, I went to counselling. I was in a dark, dark place, and wasn't sure I'd ever get out of it. My counsellor reminded me of the importance of celebrating the smaller things in life. Whether it's just getting out of bed in the morning or reaching a goal I'd been working towards, she encouraged me to celebrate when I'd achieved something. This is something that I continue to do because celebrating the small things makes you feel good when you feel small.

I took things one step further and began to break my goals down into smaller chunks. Writing a finished novel turned into a first draft or a first chapter. A published blog post turned into a plan.

When I first started doing this, I had no idea that it was a scientifically proven tactic. I had no idea that there were books written on this subject or that it was a tactic used by the British Cycling Team[5].

And then I read *Black Box Thinking*[6]. The book looks at how we handle failure, and how this has a huge affect on what we achieve in life. And it gave a name to my tactic of breaking goals down into smaller chunks: marginal gains.

With marginal gains, you break a project or long-term goal into smaller, easier-to-digest chunks. These small chunks may seem inconsequential at first, but they each push you a step closer to your goal. A book becomes a series of chapters or scenes; an essay becomes sections or paragraphs. You can break your project down as small as you like. In fact, the smaller you break it down, the better.

Give yourself a pat on the back once you achieve one of your targets. For every 1,000 words, watch an episode of your favourite TV show, or eat your favourite food. Whatever you choose for your reward, it has to be something that you really, *really* love. The stronger your love of it, the more you'll come to associate that feeling with writing.

Don't put 'finish the book' on your to-do list. Start with something smaller and more specific, such as 'character biography for Hollie', or 'character biography for Fayth'. That way, you get to tick things off more often. Ticking things off fills us with dopamine[7], also known as the happy chemical in our brain. The more often we do this, the more often we get that warm, fuzzy feeling that dopamine gives us. That feeling is addictive. The more you accomplish, the more you *want* to accomplish.

Looking at it as a whole, a 50,000+ word manuscript is intimidating. Looking at it as 1,000 words over 50 days isn't nearly as scary. You still have plenty of time to do other things around writing those 1,000 words, and there's nothing stopping you from exceeding your target either.

1,000 words is only 16.7 words per minute if you write it in an hour. 22.2 words per minute if you write it in 45 minutes. 33.3 words per minute if you write it in half an hour.

The average person speaks at around 140 words per minute[8]. If you can speak that fast, you can think that fast. And if you can think that fast, you can train your brain to type that fast. If you prefer to write by hand, there's no reason you can't come up with your own shorthand, or use something like Pitman Shorthand.

If you prefer to work by time constraints, break your novel into chunks based on how much time you have to write each day. Work out roughly how much you can write in each session, then divide your target word count by this number. If you're not sure how long your finished project will be, research the average length for your chosen medium or genre. Epic fantasy can get away with a significantly longer word count than a children's book, for example, so be aware that your chosen genre and target audience will influence your word count.

Tune Everything Out

As mentioned earlier, recent studies have shown a link between productivity and listening to music. Stephen King favours heavy rock when he writes. Me? I listen to music that fits the character or scene that I'm writing.

Music has always been able to influence my mood. I use this to my advantage when writing. I have playlists set up for different moods, characters, and books. This helps me to channel the tone that I'm going for at that particular time. There's nothing worse than working on a sad scene and having a cheesy pop song come on. Likewise when you're writing a romantic scene the last thing you want to listen to is a break-up song.

If you don't have the time/patience/music library to create playlists for different things, Spotify and Apple Music have hundreds of playlists for different activities and moods. Whatever mood you're trying to channel, there'll be something for you.

While there are studies to back up the effectiveness of listening to music when you're trying to be productive, this doesn't work for everyone. I have a friend with a music degree, for example, who instantly begins to analyse music whenever she hears it. If this is you, you could try listening to white noise instead. White noise allows you to drain out external stimuli without the added stimulus of music.

Go Dark

Going dark is when you completely block out the real world. All notifications and devices are switched off. The only thing you focus on is what's right in front of you.

In a world that's always switched on, this is difficult to do. However, once you get used to it, you'll begrudge returning to reality.

To celebrate the publication of *What Happens in London*, I went on a spa day. I left my phone in my locker all day, and you know what? I didn't miss it. Not one bit. In fact, I begrudged returning to reality when I left. I hadn't missed anything important by going dark. The sky hadn't fallen. Everyone was still fine. But I felt different. I was more relaxed.

Since then, I've tried to leave my phone a little more often.

If you think the people around you will interrupt your writing time, don't tell them that you're writing. Many people – even our loved ones – think that it's acceptable to interrupt this time, and it's crucial that they don't. The more interruptions and distractions you have, the harder it is to concentrate, and the more difficult it is to create your routine. Make it abundantly clear to anyone likely to interrupt that you are *not* to be disturbed. Turn notifications off, put your headphones on, close the door and curtains, do whatever you need to do to completely switch off from the outside world while you write.

Dealing with Idea Overload

Ever sat at your computer and wondered which project to work on?

This is something I really struggled with after finishing *What Happens in New York.* Initially I thought I'd go straight into *What Happens in London*, but the further into it I got the more I felt like I was drowning. So much happens in that book that I needed to separate myself from the world for a little while in order to recharge before I fully engrossed myself in such an emotionally-draining project.

I decided to focus on my nonfiction instead.

I completed a first draft of *Productivity for Writers* but then felt lost again. I couldn't go back to it yet – I needed to do more research and let it stew for a while – but what should I do next? My email course? A poetry collection? A *What*

Happens in New York spin-off? Back to *What Happens in London*? I couldn't decide. My mind was pulling me in so many directions and I didn't know which to take.

The best thing to do when your writing stresses you out like this is to relax. Take a bath. Read a book (unrelated to your writing). Do some exercise. (I'm sorry. I hate exercise too, but it DOES help. I only say it because it's true.) Whatever your way of relaxing is, do it. You'll be surprised how many good ideas you have when you stop overthinking everything.

Look at the ideas that you have, even if they're unfinished. Which sounds the most fun? Writing something you enjoy is important.

Now think back to your end goal and work backwards. What can you focus on in the short term that will help you to achieve it?

If you're a poet and you want to put together a collection, it may be looking at your poems to find a particular theme that you can write more poems around. If you're a novelist or screenwriter but don't know which idea to focus on, start with the easiest project. The more complicated your writing project is, the more tempting it is to put it off. Writing any novel is a huge commitment, but if you plan for your first novel to be an epic fantasy on the same scale as Tolkien, or even a young adult fantasy like Harry Potter, you're adding a huge amount of work to an already heavy workload. I'm not saying that you shouldn't write it, but you need to be prepared for the extra work ahead. Making your first writing project a high-concept epic fantasy series is like baking a Sachertorte as your first cake. Don't be afraid to start small and work your way up to more complex ideas. The first book you finish doesn't have to be the first book you publish.

If you write nonfiction or journalism, start by deciding which publications you want to submit your work to. Look at what topics they cover, and how you could write something for their audience. Compile a list of topics and go from there. Extra points if you can write something topical.

If you're like me and you write a little bit of everything, that's when things get complicated. You really need to be disciplined here. For now, you need to pick a focus. As we looked at earlier, working on multiple projects at once means you'll take longer to finish things and won't progress as quickly. Choosing something to focus on allows you to share your work with people sooner. When I had to make this decision, I chose my fiction. I had the clearest vision for it, and I was more invested in it than my poetry or nonfiction. I continued to write poetry and nonfiction when I needed a break, but most of my writing time was spent on my fiction.

Dealing with the overwhelm that comes with having too many ideas can be difficult. But think yourself lucky: I've had far more people reach out to me saying they have no ideas than saying that they have too many. Having a surplus of ideas means that you can always be creating, and as soon as you've finished one project, you can move on to the next.

Methods to Capture Your Madness

A couple of years ago, I decided to write a novel by hand. I wanted a break from staring at a screen all the time, but I wanted to keep writing, so I bought a new notebook (yellow, with typewriters on), did no planning whatsoever, and let my novel evolve organically. A couple of chapters in, I started to get ideas for later on in the book. But it was too early to put them in, so I had to force myself to keep writing scenes I wasn't feeling just to get to those key points.

I got about 6,000 words in before I gave up and went back to typing.

Writing by hand – and chronologically – just didn't work for me.

If you write by hand then type up your work, you double your work load. *Especially* if you type your work up as soon as you've finished each chapter. At least if you type it up when you've finished the manuscript you can view it as a whole and it becomes easier to edit as you go along.

If you really want to write by hand and work on a chapter at a time, you could get someone else to type it up. That way, you still have time to spend on other things. However, writing by hand just isn't an efficient use of time, especially not when it will have to be digitised eventually anyway.

Dictation is another tactic that more and more writers are using. This is especially handy if you're prone to self-editing or suffer from health problems that make it difficult to write. Everyone from Winston Churchill to bestselling authors Dan Brown and Kevin J. Anderson[9] have used dictation to write early drafts of their work. Walking about can be a good way to get the brain going, which is why Churchill liked to walk around (or take a bath!) while dictating to his secretary[10]; it's also why Steve Jobs was a fan of walking meetings[11], and why some authors like to take long, country walks while dictating their work into their phone or a recorder. Dictation allows you to walk, exercise, or even do chores while working on your first draft. It gets you away from the keyboard and can therefore help with conditions such as RSI, back pain, and fibromyalgia. It's also useful if you type slowly (although a faster typing speed will come with practise, I promise).

Macs and PCs have built-in dictation software that transcribes what you say as you speak. This cuts out the need for you or someone else to have to transcribe your writing, but as you have to tell it to add in punctuation marks, it feels odd at first. It can also be awkward if you write something that is dialogue-heavy or where punctuation is key to expressing a certain point, such as in poetry.

The beauty of dictation, though, is that you can do it anywhere. It doesn't matter how well your body or fingers function – so long as you can speak, you can dictate. All you need to get started is a phone, which many of us carry with us on a daily basis.

When you dictate your book there's no backspace or delete key. The device you record on remembers everything. You can't edit as you go with dictation – everything gets fixed later.

Interestingly, I find I'm more self-conscious when I dictate than when I type, but that could be because I'm not used to it. The speech recognition software that I tried also couldn't keep up with how fast I speak, so I had to keep stopping for it to catch up. This gave me more time to think about what I'd said and therefore more time to question it. If I found myself unable to type for prolonged periods of time I'd give it another chance, but I love the sound of fingers against keys, and writing first drafts is my favourite part of the whole process, so for now I'd rather stick to typing.

I only tried the dictation software that's built into my Mac, but there are other, more advanced options out there. While these solutions can be expensive, their systems adapt to how you speak, you can add words to their dictionary, and the more you use them, the faster they learn.

There is no right or wrong way to write. We all have our preferences. You should write in the way that feels the best for you. If, for you, that's sat by the fire with a pen and paper, go for it; if it's sat in a cafe with your laptop, do it; if it's walking through the forest with your dog, dictating your book as you stroll, then do that. Write somewhere you're fully relaxed and immersed in your idea. That way, it's easier for you to tap into your creativity and you're less likely to second-guess yourself.

Write Away

Free writing is a concept I used to find laughable. That is, until I started working full-time and realised I needed to make the most of the few hours I had each day to spend with my characters. I began to free write without even realising it. For an hour or two each evening, my characters had my full attention. Nobody else. There was no inner editor, no television, no conversations with friends in that time. There was just my characters and me.

If you've ever kept a diary, you'll have done some free writing even if you didn't realise it at the time. When you write in a diary, you write unfiltered, tapping into your subconscious to write down your innermost thoughts. If you can free write in your diary, why can't you use the same system to write other things, too?

Learning to get the idea down first and edit second is one of the toughest challenges you'll face as a writer. Switching too often between writing and editing mindsets – particularly if you write longer content – can be harmful to your creativity, though. When you edit as you write, you become overly critical of yourself. You second-guess every decision you make. Your writing process takes longer because you're not sure if this decision or that decision is the right one. When you edit as you go along, you doubt yourself before you've even given your idea any chance to grow. You tell yourself that your words aren't good enough. But you've only just written them. How can you possibly know? You're still far too close to them to view them objectively.

It doesn't matter how bad your first draft is – you have the idea down. You can fix everything else later. You can even forgo punctuation if you really want. After all, it's only a first draft.

It's not so easy when someone tells you to sit down and

free write, though. I've always struggled with writing at workshops. Even now, if I'm in a workshop and the leader asks us to write about a particular topic for a set amount of time, I'm uncomfortable. When people are around me, I want to talk to them, not write. For me, people are distractions. Not to mention when you put someone in a workshop setting then tell them to free write, it puts them on the spot. Still, sometimes these exercises can have interesting results if you give them enough of a chance.

You need to be comfortable and relaxed when you free write or you'll struggle. That's why I spend so much of my writing time at home with my headphones on.

Don't put too much pressure on yourself during your first few free writing sessions. Give yourself a simple goal – either five minutes or five hundred words – and stop when you reach that goal. You can build on it as you get used to the process.

When you get the words down and edit later, you learn to trust yourself. You teach yourself that your writing isn't as bad as you think. You tell that little voice of self-doubt that you *are* good enough. Any issues can be fixed later.

To get started free writing, you need a pen and paper, your computer, or a device to dictate into. If you use a computer, learn to touch type as it'll be faster. Have a clear goal – based on the plan you've created – before you start, and a rough idea of what you want to write about. Even if you don't know where the journey will take you, knowing the destination makes writing sessions easier and more productive.

Don't force yourself to write about something you're not interested in. Your free writing sessions will be far more productive if you write something you care about.

Over to You

When your mind is focused on a million different things, it can be difficult to sit down and write. Writing requires time, focus, and patience. If you can't focus, you'll never get anywhere.

What stops you from focusing? Is it family problems? Anxiety? Work problems? Make a list of all the things that are bothering you. Address the ones where you can talk to the person/people concerned. For example, if you're having problems in your relationship, talk it out with your partner, and don't stop until you reach a conclusion. A conclusion that fixes things, not an argument where one of you gives up/shuts down. Resolve as many issues as you can.

Have a long, hard think about the problems that you can't resolve. Why can't you resolve them? Are they out of your control? If they are, it's time for you to find a way to move on.

If you truly can't move on, how can you adapt? What changes can you make to your lifestyle that will allow you to feel more relaxed and able to write more? It could involve getting up fifteen minutes earlier, exercising more, or sacrificing your nightly TV shows so that you can do more writing.

If there's someone in your life that you have issues with but can't talk to, writing can help you to deal with your problems. Addressing your issues in fiction or poetry helps, but writing a letter to that person helps even more. Don't worry about sending it, just write as honestly as you can. The more candid you are, the more it will help you.

When you've finished your letter, discard it. If you've typed it, don't save it. If you've handwritten it, rip it up. Burn it. Scrunch it up and toss it into the recycling. Whatever makes you feel good.

HOW TO WRITE MORE

Great writing isn't just about the words on the page. To write something that truly connects with your readers, there are things *around* your writing that you need to do, too. All of these things add up to making you a better writer, a faster writer, and a more confident writer.

Whether you found an extra five minutes or five hours from the activities in the previous chapters, all of these chunks add up over the course of a week, month, and year. Five extra minutes everyday equates to 1825 minutes over a year, or over a day of extra time for your writing. Use these micro-moments to your advantage and don't ever think that you're not getting anywhere just because you only have a short amount of time to work on things each day.

Be Curious

We all know how important research is for scientific or academic writing, but have you ever thought about how important it is to your fiction, or even your poetry?

What kind of project you're working on will influence

which type(s) of research are most effective. You may find imagery, quotations, or even articles useful for your novel or poem, but that's not to say quantitative data can't be useful too – I once wrote a poem *inspired* by statistics. Anything can act as a creative trigger if you keep an open mind.

Learning new things keeps our brains active as we get older, helping us to stay happy[1] and possibly even fight off dementia (the jury's still out on that one). What do you talk about if it's not what you've learned, or what you plan to learn? Even if all you've learned is the backstory of a new character from *Eastenders*, you've still learned *something*. (Although I would highly recommend learning something like a new skill, rather than just memorising the details of a character from *Eastenders*.)

Think about your work in progress. What areas do you need to research? The origins of unicorns? Greek myths? Australian soap operas? How the body changes during the menopause? The male hormonal cycle? The list of things you could need to research for your work in progress is almost endless, but the more research you do, the more prepared you are. The more prepared you are, the harder it is to get stuck. Getting stuck comes from a lack of ideas, but if you're surrounded by images, articles, statistics, interviews and more, it's a lot harder to fall into this trap.

When it comes to doing your research, you have two options: do the research yourself (primary research), or correlate other people's research (secondary research). When you do research yourself, it's far easier to tailor results to what you need. For example, if you want to write about the Peak District, you'll be able to describe it in far more depth if you've been there yourself, taken some photos, talked to the locals, and really got a feel for what life is like in that area.

It's always better to go to the locations you write about yourself, but that isn't always possible. With secondary research, you wouldn't visit the Peak District, but you might look at images online or read what other people have said about it in the past. This will still give you a feel for what it's like, but how much of a feel you get will depend on how long you spend researching it.

When it comes to writing, you never know what you're going to need to research. If you know at least some of the areas you'll need to be knowledgeable on, it helps to do as much research as you can *before* you start. Visit the places you need to visit; read as much as you can; bookmark the most useful websites; talk to people you need to talk to (although if you have to wait for a response, you may as well just get on with things and you can fix any errors in editing).

Bullet point your notes somewhere that's easy to refer back to. Bullet points instead of lengthy paragraphs make your notes easier to skim through when you need a quick refresher. However, if you feel that writing your notes into paragraphs makes them easier to remember, do that first. Writing things in prose first can be useful if you're trying to get your head around a new idea, or working out an issue. Finding or coming up with a metaphor to explain a new concept is also a useful way to get your head around something.

Jodi Picoult has researched everything from the Holocaust and its survivors to elephant sanctuaries to autism. This research helps to immerse both her and her readers in the characters' worlds. Speaking to people who live or work in a particular industry will give you more information than any other form of research beyond experiencing it yourself, so if you can, it's worth doing.

Nurses, doctors, lawyers, and other professions can be very useful for literary research. If you know someone who works in an area you're writing about, talk to them! Most people are more than happy to share their knowledge if you ask.

If you don't know someone with knowledge about the area you're working on, online forums and social media can be great places to get advice that's tailored to your characters. These online platforms can also help you to network with people who may be useful for future writing projects, too.

The internet makes research easier than it's ever been. However, it's easy for false information to be spread online. Make sure to fact-check your sources, especially if you're writing creative nonfiction, a journalistic piece, or even a blog post. When it comes to fiction and poetry, you can get away with a certain amount of creative license. How much you can get away with will depend on the genre in which you write. Fantasy readers will be far more forgiving than a literary audience.

If you really want to immerse yourself in your character's

career or hobby, there are magazines that specialise in every interest you could possibly think of and then some. Your local bookstore will have a wide selection and may also have magazines from abroad. Most magazines also allow you to buy back issues from their website, and those that don't often post their older articles online. This means that if there's a particular area they've covered in a previous issue, you should still be able to find what you need. If not, it's highly likely the same topic has been covered elsewhere.

If you'd rather watch a documentary than read a magazine, there are documentaries on a lot of topics, too.

Inevitably, you'll find more things that you need to research as you write. There's no way you can know everything about everything before you start. So that you don't break up your writing time, make a note of what you need to research (leave a gap in your project if you have to), then go back to it when you have time to do some research.

There's no right or wrong answer when it comes to the best research method. Do what is most accessible to you, but don't be afraid to push yourself either. If you're uncomfortable reaching out to people but know of someone who has the answers that you need, why not contact them? What have you got to lose? If they say yes, you have the answers that you need, and if they say no, it's one more rejection to add to what will become a very long list that you can laugh about one day.

Read, Read, READ!

There's a huge difference between just plain reading, and reading actively. When you read actively, you learn from what you read. You learn about structure, control of language, points of view, and much, much more. You learn what makes writing work, and what makes it fall flat. You can learn just as much about these things from books you don't enjoy as you can from books that you love.

It's important to know what your competitors are doing, but you can learn how to rival your competitors by discovering what writers from other genres do, too. Never say that you don't like a particular genre or medium. There will always be something that's an exception to your rule if you look hard enough.

Any writer who tells you they don't read at least books in their genre is naive. Great painters learn from their predecessors. Great songwriters learn from their predecessors. Writers are no exception. We are not special snowflakes. We learn from those around us, and from those better than us. Reading is one of the best ways we can do this.

When you read work from people who are better writers than you (and there will always be someone who's a better writer than you), you grow as a writer. Look to writers who are strong in areas where you're weak. Analyse and annotate key passages. If something inspires you, run with it.

If you're not sure on the kinds of things you're weak on, ask your editor or beta readers. Keep your questions as specific as possible. You could even give them a questionnaire and ask them to rate your skills 1-10. The more targeted your questions are, the more useful the information you get will be.

When you know what areas you need to work on, here are some things that will help: if you want to tighten your writing and prevent purple prose (or, as I like to call it, 'frilly knicker writing'), read some young adult or children's fiction, or blog posts. All of these forms of writing need to get to the point and fast. The more frills they add, the more likely they are to lose their audience. Children and teenagers have short attention spans. Blog readers, meanwhile, can find the same information on dozens of sites. They won't stick around on yours if somewhere else has written about the same topic in a way that's more interesting or easier to understand.

Poetry helps with metaphors, similes, and imagery. Fantasy and science fiction are great for world building (even if the world you're building isn't fantasy or science fiction). Romance or women's fiction is perfect if you want to work on your characters' relationships. Crime, mystery, or thriller will help you work on your plots.

Of course, there are exceptions to these rules. You may find a poem that helps you with your structure, or a self-help book that helps you with your metaphors.

The most important thing is that you read, and you read avidly.

How to read more

Set a Realistic Target

Start by setting yourself a realistic target. If you're not a fast reader, a book a week isn't achievable. You know what time you have and roughly how long it takes you to finish a book. The more you read, the faster you'll be able to read, but in the meantime, make sure your goal is attainable.

If you haven't read for a while or if you're used to staring at a computer screen, don't expect to read the whole of *A Game of Thrones* in one sitting. Break the book down into smaller sections instead. It could be by the number of pages in the book, the number of chapters, or the period of time you have to read each day. Read until you've reached your page number, finished a chapter, or your time is up. If you still feel OK, keep going. If the words are merging together, close the book and go do something that doesn't involve a staring at a screen or looking at words on a page. Your eyes will gradually get used to looking at the page and you'll slowly be able to increase how long you can read for.

To really challenge yourself, set a goal for how many books you want to read in a year (or until the end of the year). Work out the average length of time it takes you to read a book, then divide that by the number of months, weeks, or days in a year (depending on what your average length of time is). For example, if you can read an average of one book every two weeks, that works out at 24 books in a year.

Free Up Some Time

We all waste time doing things we don't need to do. You should have an idea of exactly what time you have from the activity in How Much Time Do You Really Have?, so use that as a guide to work out when you can fit in some reading time. Once you're in a routine of reading at a particular day/time, it will become much easier.

It doesn't have to be a large amount of time. If you haven't read for a while, it's probably better to ease yourself in by reading in ten or fifteen minute chunks throughout the day. The daily commute, waiting in line for the weekly shop, or even waiting in the queue for the public loo are all perfect times to sneak in a couple of minutes' reading. This is also where ebooks come in handy, as you can always have one with you on your phone.

Track Your Progress

Using a notebook, you can keep a list of what you've read, what you want to read, and write down any thoughts on what you've ready. The sooner you update it after finishing something, the more you'll be able to remember, so try to update it while a book is still fresh in your mind.

If you prefer to type, you could use a document on your computer or phone, or even one hosted in the cloud (such as in Google Docs or Notes). The great thing about this method is that they're accessible wherever you are, so if you're on holiday and don't have room for a book journal or notebook, you can still make notes on what you've read.

Goodreads, a social network for book lovers, is another tool that you can use to track your reading. It allows you to keep track of what you want to read, what you're reading, and what you've read. You can also follow your friends or people you find interesting, leave reviews, take part in quizzes and, most importantly, set yourself reading targets.

If you're on Twitter, there's also the hashtag #amreading.

Learn From Those Wiser Than You

A lot of people – both writers and non-writers – seem to believe you can either write, or you can't. This is nonsense. You *can* teach writing, and you *can* get better at it. This is why people spend thousands on creative writing courses, books, and any other resources that claim to make them a better writer. If it's not possible to improve, if you can either write or you can't, then why are these things so popular?

To put it simply, because they work.

Not all of them do, of course. Some are better than others. The same is true in every industry.

Many courses will let you try out a module or two for free. This allows you to get a feel for the teacher's style and the kinds of things you'll learn. There's no point taking a course if you can't stand the teacher's voice or don't like their course materials.

Speak to people you know who might be familiar with the resource you're looking into and see what they thought of it. The most popular resources are often well-known in their industry.

Also, most writers these days have blogs and are more than happy to share their insights. Blogs are a great – and free – way to learn new skills. There are countless blogs out there on every topic you can think of, so there will almost always be somewhere that's covered what you need.

If you can't find what you're looking for, though, you may have to resort to the old fashioned way: books. Many of us (myself included) still prefer to get our information from books. It's a lot more difficult to get distracted reading a book than a blog post, and books often offer more insight than a blog post. Books are a great way to learn new skills and everyone from Bill Gates[2] to Warren Buffett to Oprah Winfrey are huge readers. These are very busy people, yet they find time in their day to read no matter what. If that doesn't demonstrate just how effective reading is to you, nothing will.

Be sure to pick a combination of ways to sharpen your skills. Sometimes an in-person workshop is more effective than a webinar series, whereas in other cases a webinar series might be the perfect option.

We all learn in different ways, so if you don't enjoy a course that a fellow writer recommended, chalk it up to experience and move on to your next way to learn.

Know Your Characters

Everything we write needs characters. The more the reader connects with these characters, the more powerful your writing will be. Even if your writing doesn't have people in it, animals, inanimate objects, and even scenery can become characters if their story is told in the right way. The cars in *Back to the Future* and *Supernatural* are prime examples of this.

When writing, it's imperative to know everything about your characters. You may not need to use everything, but that doesn't matter. The more you know about them, the easier it is to really get into their heads, and the easier they are to write about. Because you have a deeper connection with them, your readers will, too.

Once you know why your character is so interesting, you need to show your readers. Even if they don't seem like a particularly nice person (like Darth Vader, for example), there still needs to be something that humanises your character and helps your audience to connect with them. Darth Vader may be evil, but he started out just like the rest of us. He wanted what was best for his family. When he lost that, his anger pushed him towards the dark side. The anger at losing a loved one is something we can all relate to, and while we may not all turn to the dark side because of it, it's backstories like this that help us to connect to even the most evil of characters.

The way a character speaks can not only reflect who they are as a person, but also help to differentiate them from other characters within your story. Do they have an accent? Do they use a particular dialect? Do they have their very own idiolect?

The subtext of what they say is particularly important. Take, for instance, a marriage proposal: 'Will you marry me?' is a question. It shows respect; it could show nerves. It could even show traditionalism or that the proposer has got down on one knee. 'Marry me,' meanwhile, is a statement. It's not a question – it almost sounds like a demand. From some characters, it could be. Perhaps the proposer thinks highly of themselves? That the other person would be lucky to marry them? It also seems more spontaneous than the question, don't you think? 'We should get married,' unlike the other two, is more of a suggestion. Almost an off-the-cuff remark that could be said by someone who may or may not have put much thought into it. 'Let's get married!' meanwhile, could be said as an exclamative, or could be more along the lines of, 'Let's get married.' This is definitely a spontaneous proposal. It's not a question, but it's not a demand either. Those four remarks would be said by four very different people. They also say a lot about the people who has said them, and they've probably saved you about ten pages of personality description. It's also explained your character in a far more interesting way. Just because you don't read excessively into what your characters say, that doesn't mean that your readers won't. Or that you shouldn't.

The slightest anomaly in your character can say more than a biography of their whole life if done right. Small clues allow your reader to play Sherlock Holmes and work out for themselves what kind of person your character is.

However, whatever you write, each person will read your work slightly differently. Some people will read between the lines of one thing and not another. If they read your writing more than once, they may pick up on different things each time. That doesn't mean you need to be obvious in what you write in order to steer the reader towards a particular conclusion, but it does mean you need to think about your reader when you edit your work. Not everything will come across as you intended it to when you wrote it.

If you're stuck for where to begin with a character, try basing them on someone you know, such as a close friend. Be sure not to base them *too* closely though – you don't want to offend anyone. After a while, your character will start to become their own person, and the more you create new characters, the less you'll need to trigger your creative juices.

Never Say You Have Writer's Block

How many times have you said that you've got writer's block? Aloud, written down, thought to yourself. Take a moment and really think about it.

Now think about how many times you've told yourself that you can write.

I'm going to assume that the former outnumbers the latter.

If it doesn't, you can skip this section.

If it does, read on.

Writer's block manifests itself differently for everyone. For some it may also involve only writing rubbish (subjective), or not being able to work out a particular issue. It's an excuse I used to use a lot. If I had an assignment to turn in and I didn't like what I'd written, I'd say, 'I have writer's block. It's not my fault it sucks.' If a friend asked to read the next chapter of a story I was working on but I had no idea what to write next, I'd fob them off: 'I have writer's block. I don't know when it'll be.' If I had a blog post to write and didn't know what to write about, instead of doing some research, I'd decide I had writer's block and it was a justifiable excuse to let my readers down. I'd try to blame my lack of writing on some ethereal disease. An ethereal disease that doesn't exist.

That's right.

I said it.

Writer's block doesn't exist.

Writer's block is a prime example of the power of the mind: the more you tell yourself you have writer's block, the more you'll believe it.

You find things to reinforce your state of writer's block, like not being able to come up with a character name, find the right word to describe something, or not knowing what happens next. Then you dismiss what you've written as rubbish because of an increasing pile of small things that add up. This is called confirmation bias – where we look for things that reinforce something we already believe. It's regularly used in politics and religion.

Writer's block often comes from believing that everything we write has to be perfect. Even published writers have some books that are better than others. What's important is that they never stop writing. If they stop, it becomes harder to get back into, just the same as when you stop lifting weights, you need to restart with lighter weights.

When you get paid to write, for instance if you're a journalist or copywriter, you can't afford to have writer's block. You have deadlines to meet. Deadlines aren't negotiable because you can't put the words onto the page. Even if your first draft really does suck – and if you get paid to write, there will be times your boss or client says just that – at least you have something that you can work on. You've fought through that mental blockage to get to the other side and find some words, even if they're not the ones you want.

If you've written a tweet or a text or even an email today, you've written *something*. If you've held a conversation today, you've had a coherent thought that you could've written down if you'd wanted to. These things all count. When you do these things, you're already halfway towards creating something.

Do you overthink every tweet, text, or email that you send? Every conversation that you have? Didn't think so. There's no reason you shouldn't treat your other forms of writing in the same way. Get your idea down. You can fix everything else later.

Get your creative juices flowing

Don't be afraid to push yourself by writing things you're unfamiliar with. Write a sonnet or a children's story. Write political satire or a haiku. Try as many different writing styles as you can, and when you've tried everything you can think of, research some more. The more writing styles you experiment with, the closer you'll get to finding your voice. I've met many people who say they can't/don't write poetry, then when they do write it find that they enjoy it and it's not as difficult as they thought. Had they not given poetry a chance, they never would've discovered this. Don't be one of those people.

Even if you find you don't like a particular style or medium, try a different one. Just because you're not keen on writing for children, that doesn't mean you'll feel the same about writing for young or new adults. Just because sonnets aren't your thing, that doesn't mean that free verse isn't.

Another way to flex your writing muscles is to switch from typing to pen and paper or dictation. Doing so can help you to clarify your ideas. Sometimes, though, you're just not ready to write something. Even with a perfectly adequate plan, pieces don't always work and there's no obvious reason why. I once wrote a blog post about celebrity relationships, but even with research and planning, it didn't work. Then a celebrity couple broke up, and BOOM! There was my opening. The piece worked better because it was topical.

When you're struggling with an idea, give yourself time to let it develop. Not every idea will develop like a digital photograph – some develop more slowly, like an analogue photograph in a dark room. For some ideas, you may need to wait for current events to occur. These will strengthen your piece and make readers more interested in the subject, but they also give you less time to write about the subject as readers move on quickly.

Not every idea will manifest itself to you in full the minute you put your fingers to the keyboard. Give yourself a break and don't put too much pressure on yourself.

If you know how part of your piece will look but it's not

the start, write from there. There's nothing wrong with starting your first draft in the middle, or even at the end. First drafts are where you cut out the pieces based on your plan. Editing is where you tack and sew your project together, and copyediting and proofreading are when you add in the darts and hem the edges. If you don't write chronologically, nobody will know! As long as your finished piece makes sense, nobody will care, either.

Write in a way that you're comfortable with, and if that means writing the ending first and the beginning last, then do it.

Stop Editing as You Write

Fear of writing badly is probably the number two excuse I've heard people use not to write (number one is self-doubt, and this is tied to that in a way). They're afraid to write something that sucks, and they convince themselves that everything they write sucks, so instead of finding a way to fix their sucky writing, they just don't write at all.

This is disastrous for many reasons. For starters, you'll only get better at writing with practise. And there's no way you're going to be able to practise if you're not writing.

When you start learning a new skill, or you're at the beginning of your writing journey, you're going to suck. Even if you started writing at a young age, if you don't practise regularly you won't be as good as someone the same age as you who practised everyday.

But that's OK.

Practise is your friend.

There's no law that says you *must* show everyone – or in fact, show *anyone* – your first draft. There also isn't a law that says the first draft of your work in progress is the work you'll be remembered for.

First drafts should be for getting down the vision that's in your head, no one else's. When you start to cloud your vision with other people's thoughts and opinions, your plot, style, and tone can change dramatically.

Don't pressurise yourself to write a perfect first draft. Your first draft is only the foundation of your house; each subsequent draft is a wall or a ceiling. Copyediting is the plaster on the walls and proofreading is the interior decoration. And much like when you build a house, you can't do all these things at once. But if you put the work in, you can build a truly brilliant house.

It doesn't matter if you misspell a word in your first draft. Your friends know you can spell it. You know you can spell it. You can fix it when you return to edit it. If it bothers you that much, and it's something you do often with certain words, train yourself to stop mistyping it. When I was a teenager, I often typed 'teh' instead of 'the'. My friends knew what I meant, but it bugged me. So I decided that each time I typed 'teh', I would retype the whole sentence. My fingers soon learned how to type the letters in the right order.

When it comes to larger edits – such as changing an entire paragraph or plot point – ask yourself why you feel the need to do it before you've finished writing. Is it a crucial plot point that needs to change so that the rest of the story can get to a certain point? Is it a pivotal scene?

Every scene in your story must work for its place, but when you're working on a first draft, it's better to have too many words than too few. It's a lot easier to cut out excess words than it is to add content in.

The next time you start self-editing, think about how much time you're wasting. For every minute you spend dwelling over a word or phrase, that's one less paragraph you could've written.

If you find yourself stuck on something, for instance the name of a new character, rather than dwell on it and break up your writing session, use a placeholder such as a dash, comment, or asterisk, then go back to it. Alternatively, you could refer to them by their role in the story, such as 'the manager' or 'the waiter'.

Name as many characters as you can before you start your writing project. Try to get a little bit of an idea of what they're like, but don't go too crazy – you'll find out new things about them as you go, and the more you write about your characters, the more you'll realise what kinds of people they are.

Keep a list of names you've used and a list of names you haven't, that way you don't repeat them and have a reference list of your favourites if you're stuck.

There will be plenty more things that threaten to break up your writing time, from the that niggling voice of self-doubt to a crucial topic you forgot to research. Don't let these things get in your way.

Your writing and editing time should be kept far, far away from each other. Writing and editing require very different mindsets, and the more you flit between the two, the more difficult it is to focus on one. When you're working on shorter projects such as a blog post or a poem, this isn't as much of a problem, but if you're working on longer pieces such as a screenplay or a novel, constantly switching between writing and editing means you're always second guessing your decisions. Trust yourself to run with your idea until you reach the end. Then, after you've separated yourself from your project for at least a few days – preferably a few weeks – return to it and start editing.

Editing is an important skill to have, but it's a completely different mindset to writing. Many full-time editors I've worked with have stopped writing altogether because they've either found that they enjoy editing more, or they don't like switching between the two.

As writers, we all keep some things in our stories for our own amusement – such as J.K.Rowling wanting Ron and Hermione together[3] – but there are times when this feels awkward and unnatural to the reader. J.K.Rowling has fully admitted she shouldn't have ended the Potter books how she did. She'd change them if she wrote them now. But at the time, it was what she wanted to do. She wasn't prepared to kill her darlings. But, as writers, we must.

Just not until we've finished that first draft.

How to stop yourself from editing as you write

If you find yourself editing as you write, many of the tactics in the free writing section will help you. Free writing is the opposite of editing as you write, so it's a good way to get into the habit of trusting your instincts. Remember not to sit down for a long writing session if you're not used to it. You'll be far more productive and get used to the process faster if you start off small.

The most important thing you need to do to truly stop yourself from editing as you write is to completely immerse yourself in what you're writing. Many of my friends have remarked that I talk about my characters like they're real people. That's because, to me, they are. They've been floating around in my head everyday for almost a decade. Talking about them is as easy for me as it is to talk about Boyfriend or Mum and Nan. I can go shopping and point out clothes that the characters would wear or find ugly (and have done in the past). They frequently offer commentary on my everyday life, too. This may make me sound slightly nuts, but when you're a fiction writer, it's beneficial.

The more immersed you are in what you write, the easier it is to write freely. You don't think about what you're writing because you're so desperate to spend time with your characters that you pour everything onto the page in the same way that you would if you were writing in a diary about your best friends. Ultimately, you should know your characters better than your best friends, because unlike your real-life friends, they're your creations. Nobody will ever know them better than you do. If you don't know anything about them, how can you expect anyone else to?

Planning out what you write further helps to prevent you from second-guessing your decisions because you've already made the most important ones for the scene you're writing.

A little self-awareness helps, too: if you can type 100wpm and you stop to think about a sentence you've just written for a couple of minutes, you've written 200 fewer words than you could have. Would you rather dwell on those words now, while the idea is still fresh in your head, or would you prefer to think about them when they've had chance to stew and you can view them more objectively? With a little practise, self-awareness can help you to break your bad habits. You have to really and truly want to break your bad habits in order to be successful, though.

Save Everything

When I was a teenager, I would only save the writing that I really felt was worth saving. If, at the end of a writing session, I didn't like what I'd written, I wouldn't save any of it. If I didn't like something – whether it was a poem, short story, or even a chapter of a novel – I was too embarrassed to even have it saved on my hard drive.

Fast-forward ten years, and I save *everything*.

You never know what crappy idea will be the springboard for your next great idea. You may hate something now, but when you return to it in a few months' time, find a word or a phrase that inspires something else. You may even find it's not as terrible as you initially thought.

Every word you write is part of your writing journey and can lead you to your greatest project yet. If you don't save everything, you have no record of your progress.

Some ideas will take you years to finish. Don't worry. No word you write is ever wasted because it all leads you further down the path to becoming a better writer. Even a failed novel can turn into a bestseller when rewritten. You'll never know if you dismiss an idea in the heat of the moment. Don't let that fleeting moment control you. Future you will think differently to present you, just the same as present you thinks differently to past you. The more you push yourself, the more you'll change and marvel at how far you've come.

The only person you should ever compete with is your past self. If you don't feel you've achieved as much as you could have, take stock, then continue on and push yourself harder.

If you've achieved lots, well done! Now keep going.

Embrace Critique

It doesn't matter hold old we are – we all have to accept critique. Some people deliver it tactfully, while others are as subtle as a cricket bat to the face. It's far easier to digest critique from those who do it tactfully, but not everyone in life does.

Some people who critique your work come from a positive place. They tear it apart so that you can rebuild it stronger. The worst critique is no critique. When you receive nothing but tumbleweeds, it's a sign that the person who's read (or was supposed to read) your work doesn't care. They don't want to help you become a better writer. They're indifferent to you.

On the other hand, listening to someone tear apart your writing can hurt, especially if you're not used to it. Before you react or respond, take some time to digest the comments. If you're meeting in person, pause and think before you respond. It's easy to lose your temper at someone when they've said something you disagree with, but in hindsight, you may find that they were right.

At Apple's WWDC back in 1997, Steve Jobs was told by an attendee that he didn't know what he was talking about, and asked to explain his stance[4]. Instead of getting angry or defensive, he took a few seconds, then responded calmly and acknowledged that the questioner was right about some things. Admitting that – particularly in such a public way – takes confidence. He went on to admit that he didn't know everything, and that he'd made mistakes. Even if you disagree with someone, that doesn't mean you can't still treat them with respect.

When you're a writer, the same rule still applies. Your readers have done you a favour by reading your writing. *They* do not owe *you* anything.

If the notes are written, read them, then go do something else. This time away allows you to cool off should any of the comments negatively affect your mood, and means that you can see your work more objectively when you return to it.

If the comments aren't written and people are waiting on your response, take a note from Steve Jobs's book. Pause, reflect, then respond. Don't be afraid to let your guard down. You'll learn far more if you acknowledge the criticism than if you shut it down.

Remember that no matter how critical someone is, they've taken the time to read your work. Even bad comments online can can have a positive impact as they often lead to more exposure for you.

You wake up a different person each day. The longer you separate yourself from your work in progress, the easier it is to see your creation objectively. That's why it's so important to let writing stew, and to share it with beta readers and editors.

When you return to review the comments, there are no shocks as you already know what the comments are. You're therefore more prepared to deal with them.

Learning how to handle critique is as much of a skill as writing itself. However, like everything, it can be learned. All you need is a little patience and a willingness to work with the people who can push you the hardest. It will be difficult at first, but your future readers will thank you.

Be Accountable

Pick a close, supportive friend. Tell them how and when you intend to finish your writing project. Tell them when you want your first draft to be completed, when you want to submit to beta readers, when you want the final draft complete. Give them as many deadlines as you like. But be aware that life can get in the way sometimes. Sometimes you find that you don't like what you have and need to start again. Rather than kick yourself, learn from it, and move on. That doesn't mean your deadline is flexible if you're just being lazy, though. Your deadline is flexible when you're ill, or have to care for a family member, or you lose your job. It's not negotiable when you just can't be bothered.

The friend you choose can be a fellow writer, or simply someone that's supportive. It doesn't matter. What matters is that you speak to them regularly and they can keep you on track. They can give you a nudge and a pep talk when you need it, but they won't shout at you because you missed your deadline due to a family emergency.

There are websites out there where you can pledge money to a friend or charity. If you don't reach your goal, they get the money. If you do reach it, you get to keep it. However, I'm not a fan of this for a couple of reasons. Firstly, if life gets in the way, that's really not your fault. Secondly, if you can afford to pledge money, you probably won't miss it. If you're not going to miss it, it's not enough of a motivator to push you towards your goal.

Writing groups – both online and in person – are effective at pushing you further towards your goal so long as you and your fellow writers are all on the same page. Much like you need to be on the same page for a friendship or relationship to thrive, writing groups are the same. If one of you wants to self-publish children's fiction on Amazon while the other wants to publish serious journalism in the traditional media, you're going to approach writing very differently and offer different kinds of feedback. Writers in your genre, on the other hand, or that are published in a similar way to you, will have an understanding of where you're coming from and can help you to work out how long a project will take, or how to fix issues you're facing.

Social media can be a way to find other, like-minded writers if you don't know of any already. There are Facebook groups and Twitter hashtags that cover just about everything. A quick search for the type of writing that you do and the social network you're interested in will bring up plenty of suggestions to get you started.

Jerry Seinfeld used to hold himself accountable by using a wall calendar that showed a full year on one page[5]. Every time he wrote, he put a big X on that date. Slowly but surely, he created a habit. He began to like seeing that red X on the wall. So he kept writing. Soon, he had a whole calendar full of red Xs and hundreds of jokes he may never have written otherwise.

If you adopt this tactic and put an X on a wall calendar at home, it gives you a further level of accountability as your loved ones/roommates can see what you've achieved and can give you a nudge if you haven't written on a particular day.

Create Healthy Habits

Sleep it off

Sleep is important for our brains and bodies to recharge. Our dreams can also be great inspiration for current and future projects. If it wasn't for a dream, some of my characters wouldn't exist.

While there are people out there that can survive on just a few hours of sleep a night, most adults need 7-9 hours of sleep a night to be able to fully function[6].

On the days when you don't get such a good night's sleep, never underestimate the power nap. Having twenty minutes to half an hour to allow your brain and body to recharge when it's drained can be the difference between a productive afternoon and getting nothing done. You'll wake up even more alert if you have a coffee or other caffeinated drink before you fall asleep.[7] This is because caffeine takes approximately 20 minutes to kick in, so you'll wake up just as it's starting to work.

Power naps are like using jump cables to restart your car battery – they offer a quick burst of energy when you're drained. If you sleep for longer than half an hour you risk entering a deeper sleep and waking up more tired than you were originally[8].

You are what you eat

It may seem weird to discuss diet in a book about writing and productivity, but it plays a bigger part than we sometimes realise.

Dehydration causes headaches and lethargy, making concentrating on tasks difficult. Use the recommended eight glasses of liquid a day as a guide, then adjust it based on how you feel. Different circumstances such as where you are, what medication you take, what your body's shape and size are, and what food you've eaten during the day will dictate how much you water you need to function.

A steady blood sugar is also key for productivity. When you binge on sugar, you may have a huge energy surge, but this leads to a crash a few hours later. This crash makes us feel low, grumpy, and has the opposite effect. The more sugar you've had, the harder the crash is. Instead of bingeing on sugar, try to eat more protein to keep you fuller for longer.

Healthy fats such as avocados, nuts, and olive oil also help to keep you fuller for longer, and are great for your mind and body. Fish such as salmon which is high in omega-3 is even better, and can also support memory and motor functions.

If you're prone to comfort eating, ask yourself why you do this. Eating too much can be just as damaging to your body as not eating enough or eating the wrong things. A healthy diet really is about balance. The more you look after yourself, the more you'll achieve.

Over to You

Think of your end goal. For example, publishing your book. Now break it down into smaller chunks. Finishing that first draft. Doing your first read through. Doing your first edit. Your second. Your third. Showing it to your beta readers. More edits. You get the picture.

If you write shorter pieces such as poems or blog posts, you could aim to create a collection of them on a particular theme/topic.

Now devise a timeline. Don't start at the end. Start at the beginning. Be realistic. How soon do you think you can finish that first draft? If it's in a month's time, go for a month's time. Remember to tell your accountability buddy/buddies what your deadline is so that they can make sure you stick to it. Post your deadlines on social media too if you're comfortable doing so for extra encouragement.

Plan as far ahead as you can. Make sure to think about important events like birthdays and holidays that might mean you have less time to write for a few days.

Keep your timeline somewhere safe. Put it in your computer's calendar, in your diary, on your wall calendar; anywhere that you check often. Seeing it regularly means that it's always at the forefront of your mind.

Don't worry about how long or short your timeline is. Just make sure that *everything* you have to do is on it. The smaller the task, the better. Make sure even the tiniest tasks have a completion date beside them.

If you don't achieve something by the date you'd planned to, take some time to assess why. Were you too ambitious? Did life get in the way? What can you do differently next time?

If you achieved everything sooner than you'd planned, change your dates. Push yourself harder. Don't be afraid of a little challenge. It's only when we're challenged that we really learn and grow.

TOOLS TO TRY

There are lots of tools out there that aim to help you write more, get organised, and be more productive. I've mentioned many of my favourites in this book already. Here I'm going to look at them in a bit more depth and discuss some alternatives. I've tried to include a variety of different tools to record your ideas, track your progress, and improve your grammar.

I've not been paid by any of the companies mentioned in this section – all of the opinions and experiences are my own. Prices aren't included because they could change at any time and vary from country to country, but it does say whether programs are free, subscription-based, or a one-off payment.

When using these tools, remember that the aim is to make you more productive, not less. If you already use a note-taking app, don't spend hours migrating everything over to a different application for the sake of it – do it because there's extra benefits to doing so in the long run. For example, I have over 600 notes on the Notes app on my phone. To migrate all of those over to another app would be a total waste of time. A better way to try out a different notes app would be for me to use it for new notes, or notes on a particular area, such as blog post ideas. Tools aimed at making you more productive only succeed if you don't spend more time setting them up than actually using them.

Writing Programs

Scrivener

I could rave about Literature and Latte's Scrivener until I ran out of breath. Without Scrivener, I never would've finished any of my writing projects. For the disorganised mind, Scrivener is the *perfect* tool. I don't write my first drafts chronologically – I write the most important scenes first. Scrivener allows me to write scenes in any order I like, and reorder them as many times as I like.

I love that I can compartmentalise and focus on one scene at a time without having to think about the rest of the words before or after what I'm writing. I can zoom in on that scene and drown out as much noise as I want. I can also see the bigger picture if I want to, whether that's the whole chapter, volume, or book.

It's not the easiest program to use, but it is one of the most rewarding. Scrivener also has a free trial that lasts for thirty days of *use*. This is fairly unique compared to a lot of free trials, which tend to expire after thirty days of existing on your hard drive. Thirty days is plenty of time to work out if Scrivener is right for you by experimenting with different guides and tutorials.

There are a lot of paid courses out there on how to use it, but I figured out most things from free webinars and talking to friends. Scrivener is a fairly well-known writing software these days, so you probably already know someone that uses it and is happy to show you how it works.

As well as allowing you to organise your writing, Scrivener also allows you to keep all your research files in the same project as your writing. That means instead of having dozens of research projects on your hard drive, you can keep them all in one easy-to-find location. Whether you organise your research in tables, bullet points, or imagery, you can store them all inside Scrivener's research section. It also has templates for character and place descriptions to help you really get to know the world in which your project is set.

You can back up your work automatically to a place of your choice, but these ZIP files can take up a lot of room, so be careful if you have the automatic back up feature enabled and a small hard drive/not a lot of room left in your cloud.

You can also colour-code comments and highlight sections. The iOS version also has a sleek-looking night mode for those late-night writing sessions.

Scrivener is one of the cheapest word processing programs you'll find, especially when you factor in its other features which some companies charge hundreds for.

To fully take advantage of the mobile capabilities, your projects you have to be synced with Dropbox.

Scrivener allows you to convert your books into ebook format, as well as into PDF for print, Microsoft Word,

FinalDraft, and many other formats.

Both desktop and mobile versions can be bought from the App Store if you use an Apple device, or via the Literature and Latte website for Mac or PC users.

Novlr

Novlr describes itself as 'built by writers for writers'. They add in new features weekly, and users can also suggest features they'd like to see.

It's web-based, meaning that you can work on your writing wherever you are, however it doesn't work on mobile devices. Work is stored in their cloud, but they also offer the option to backup to Google Drive or Dropbox.

Novlr has a sleek and modern interface, and in-depth tracking features. It also offers the ability to add notes to your work, and gives you the option to view a full list of the notes in your work in progress. Seeing a full list of your notes and knowing how many you have left to go through is particularly useful if you a) make a lot of notes and b) want to plan out how many notes you'll go through each day, although some notes will obviously take more time to work on than others.

Even though Novlr is web-based, you can still write in offline mode. It stores everything locally, automatically saving it to the cloud when you reconnect to the internet. If you accidentally close your browser, it remembers what you've written so that it can still save to the cloud the next time you're online.

If you like to write late at night, Novlr also has a night mode that makes it easier on your eyes.

Travelling more and having a longer commute, I can definitely see the benefit of writing using something that's cloud-based. If you flit between lots of devices, it's definitely worth looking into Novlr.

Because of the way that Novlr operates, it's a subscription-based service instead of a one-off purchase. This means that you always get new features when they're added, but if you're on a budget it may not be the best option for you long-term.

ZenPen

ZenPen is a no-frills web-based text editor which you can make fullscreen to block out everything else on your screen. It also offers titles, block quotes, hyperlinks, and the usual formatting options you'd expect from a word processor.

The handful of buttons on the left are unobtrusive and fade into the background unless you choose to use them. The buttons offer you fullscreen mode; target word count; night mode, and save.

When you're finished, you can save your work to your hard drive as Markdown, HTML, or Plain Text. However, it doesn't offer book formatting/exporting like Scrivener or Novlr does.

But the best part about ZenPen? It's free!

If you're interested in programming, you can also find out more about ZenPen over on GitHub.

Microsoft Word

Microsoft Word deserves a mention as it's used by many writers and editors, and a lot of places still expect submissions to be sent in Microsoft Word format. Up until I bought Scrivener a couple of years ago, I used it daily. I still use it for writing poems and drafts of blog posts, but I've switched to using Scrivener for longer content. Word can make longer content difficult to navigate, particularly if you don't write chronologically.

Microsoft Word comes as part of the Microsoft Office package, which you can either purchase with a one-off payment, or as an ongoing subscription to ensure you always have the latest version.

If you like the idea of Microsoft Office but don't like the price tag, Pages, Open Office, or Google Docs are free alternatives with similar features.

Progress and Goal Trackers

Diary

Even though I love using technology to boost productivity, sometimes the old fashioned way still fairs better. A diary can be updated quickly and easily, and can be flicked through at a glance. I use mine to track what writing and exercise I do each day. I also make notes on anything that might've affected my results, such as courses I've been on or my laptop breaking (which it did twice over the course of writing this book and *What Happens in London*).

There are many different versions of journaling and note

taking that you could try. I've recently started using a version of bullet journaling for my work and personal life, and have so far found it effective. I found bullet journaling itself a little too time-consuming, but I liked the idea of using symbols for different tasks, so I've adopted that.

You could also use your diary to write more in-depth insights, such as how you're feeling mentally or physically, and what you think may be the cause of that. If you struggle with free writing, this is a good way to tap into your subconscious and practise your free writing skills.

Look back through your diary regularly. Is there a pattern? What do you do on your most productive days? How do they differ from the days when you write less? Discovering your patterns means you can find ways around roadblocks and embrace the things that make you more productive.

Blog

A blog is a more public way of tracking your progress. It's up to you how much you share with your audience. However, it's worth remembering that a whole new level of work comes from running a blog, so keep that in mind if you decide to set one up. Owning your own website is about more than just content creation – particularly if you host it yourself and don't use a free platform such as WordPress.com or Blogger – and if you want your blog to reach an audience, social media and SEO are key.

Of course, it's important for writers who want to reach a wider audience to have some form of website anyway. The earlier you set it up, the more you and your readers can see your progress through your writing journey. This is great for your readers but may end up being cringeworthy for you in a few years' time. This isn't a bad thing, though! It's a sign of how much you've grown.

If you do decide to track your progress on a blog, be consistent with what you write about and when. Perhaps you could write a weekly or monthly musings post about what you've learned/researched for your work in progress, things you've discovered about your characters, words you've written, etc. The beauty of it is that it's up to you.

However, you should always think about what your readers would want first and foremost. You'll keep people coming back again and again if there's something it for them.

Social Media

One thing that people often forget about social media is that it remembers *everything*. Unless you actively go through all of your old posts and delete them, what you post will be there until the site is deleted. What you post may even outlive you.

This can be incredibly useful. If you use social media to post about your writing, you can look back through your timeline and see what you've accomplished over weeks, months, or even years. You can also keep in touch with accountability buddies or meet new ones, which can further help to keep you on track and see how far you've progressed.

Scrivener

Not only can you use Scrivener to write, but you can also use it to track your progress. You can set a target word count for a project, and a target completion date. It then calculates how many words you need to write to reach your goal in time. You can change this and give yourself a set amount of words per day if you'd prefer (mine is set to 1,000 words per day for everything I work on, regardless of when I want to finish the project and how many words I think it'll be). You'll then get a notification when you hit your target. The progress bar goes from red to orange to green the closer to your word count you get.

You can also customise your goal by telling Scrivener to count words written anywhere in the project or just your manuscript; by having your word count reset at midnight or on project close, and even by allowing it to include negative figures.

The only downside is that this awesome feature isn't available on the iOS app.

Novlr

Novlr has some of the most in-depth tracking and goal setting features I've seen. If you're new to the software, it works out how much you could write, on average, over different periods of time based on your usage so far. This proves that small writing sessions add up – even if you only write 500 words in a day, if you do that everyday for a year, you'll have written 182,500 words.

It also works out your preferred time of day to write, and how much time you spend writing during the day, month, and year.

The more you use it, the more accurate its statistics are.

Note Taking and Organisational Tools

Notebook

Many writers insist that you should carry a notebook around with you everywhere so that no matter what, you can always write down your ideas.

If you type a lot, sometimes changing things up and writing by hand can give you a new perspective on a challenge. Notebooks are also useful for checklists, doodles, and mind maps.

Notes

I swear by the Notes app on my iPhone. I regularly use it when I'm out and about, then sync everything across to my laptop when I get home. Doing this saves me a *lot* of time. I type what I'm thinking as the idea comes into my head, then when I get home I don't need to type anything up or try to remember an idea. I can write everything down there and then, then move on to something else. Notes also works with Siri, meaning that it's easy to record an idea even if you can't type.

If you've been using Notes for a while, it can be confusing to try and find what you're looking for, but more recent versions allow you to create folders and sort your notes into them. You can also separate them out and have different notes on different devices.

Notes allows you to add basic formatting such as bold, italics, checklists, etc. Copying and pasting text from Notes into sites such as WordPress doesn't affect the formatting or coding like it does from some other programs.

Evernote

Evernote allows you to make notes on your phone, tablet, or computer and sync them with your other devices. You can categorise your notes, scan in photos and receipts, and include images. Updating between devices is seamless, but I used it to draft a couple of blog posts, and when I pasted them into WordPress it added in some random coding that messed up the layout.

That being said, Evernote is a useful place to store all the different kinds of research and inspiration that you collect. Being able to sync your findings between devices also saves time and means you don't have to search your hard drive or notebooks to find something.

The basic version – which allows you to sync two devices – is free. There's also a business version available.

Bear

Bear was awarded app of the year by the App Store in 2016. It allows you to format your notes, and organise them into categories using hashtags.

For a subscription fee, you can also convert them into a variety of formats including HTML and Microsoft Word, and sync your notes between devices. It's a clean, easy-to-use app that makes organising hundreds of notes a lot easier than your average notes app.

Google Keep

Google Keep is like a noticeboard built into your browser or phone. It's great for saving links to articles or setting reminders for yourself. You can categorise what you write, add images, and add contributors too. It looks like an online pin board, so if you tend to write longer, more text-based pieces you may be better off using Notes, Evernote, or Bear, but if you want to keep organised and keep on top of things, it's worth checking out.

Google Keep is free and available as a browser extension, iOS app, and Android app.

Todoist

Todoist is the ultimate to-do list.

You can create multiple lists within your Todoist app, then have sublists for each of those. Each task you create can be assigned a due date and time. In the premium version, you can also add comments and upload files such as photos, PDFs, or spreadsheets, and set reminders.

If you'd like your accountability buddy to see what progress you've made or what you've yet to accomplish, you can share your to-do lists with a friend. This is set on a per-list basis, so it's up to you which lists you share.

My favourite part of Todoist is the ability to set recurring reminders. For example, when I first created my routine, I had a daily reminder to write my 1,000 words. I also had a fortnightly reminder to make sure I watered our houseplants (this also stopped me from overwatering them, as I knew when I'd last done it).

Todoist also integrates with the Amazon Echo.

Trello

Trello is a visual way to keep track of everything you have to do. Each project is organised into boards. You can then create lists within each board. I have a board for my blog with lists for post ideas, posts that have been written, ones that need to be edited, ones waiting for formatting, etc. You can have as many boards and lists as you like.

You can upload attachments, collaborate with other people, designate tasks, and archive the tasks that you've completed.

Trello is used by many companies to keep teams organised, but there's no reason you can't use it for your personal projects, too. It's a lot more versatile than your average list app.

Power-ups allow you to add additional features to your Trello boards. These include creating a calendar to visualise your deadlines, integration with applications such as MailChimp or Dropbox, or the ability to add GIFs to your cards. You can add one power-up to each board using the free version. A paid version is also available which has additional features and allows you to add more power-ups to your boards.

Grammar and Language Checkers

Grammarly

Grammarly is one of the most well-known grammar checkers out there. Their browser-add on proofreads what you write before you post it online. It picks up on more than Microsoft World's (awful) grammar checker, and can also work out the context of your writing.

While many people rave about Grammarly, I have to say that I've had issues with it more than once. The most recent one I found was when writing a post for social media – it suggested a sentence should read 'I followed this advise' instead of 'I followed this advice'. It also kept telling me British spellings were wrong, despite me having told it I wanted to write in British English.

AI gets more intelligent as time goes on, but it's not perfect. That's why Grammarly made the mistake above, and why Microsoft Word still struggles with 'its' and 'it's'.

If you really struggle with grammar, Grammarly is worth checking out. While I don't like it, I do know people who've found that their grammar has improved greatly from using it.

A premium version of Grammarly is available for a monthly fee which picks up on more than the free version and also has a plagiarism checker. Windows users can also take advantage of Grammarly for Microsoft Office. A free web editor is available if you don't use Windows or Microsoft Office.

Hemingway

Hemingway is one of my favourite writing tools. I've used it for everything from job applications to blog posts. You can copy and paste your writing into it, or type straight into its text editor. It will then tell you how many instances of passive voice, long sentences, and overly-complicated language you've used. Hemingway won't correct those misplaced commas or highlight any cliches, though. Because of this I'd say it's better suited to you if you've already got a grasp of the basic concepts of grammar but want to ensure you're writing in plain English to appeal to the widest audience.

The key to great writing is to make it as simple as possible. That's why Hemingway not only points out when you could use simpler words, but it also grades your writing. The lower the score, the better.

Hemingway offers a free, web-based version, as well as a paid-for desktop version that works offline and integrates with WordPress, Medium, and Microsoft Word.

After the Deadline

After the Deadline is a browser add-on for Chrome and FireFox. It checks for things like cliches, passive voice, and complex phrasing, but doesn't differentiate between the different types of English.

If you want to tighten your social media statuses it's worth considering, however I couldn't get it to work in WordPress, which is where I feel grammar-checking browser add-ons are most useful.

Browser Add-Ons

RescueTime

RescueTime is a Chrome and FireFox add-on that tracks how you *really* use the internet. It collects stats about what kinds of websites you spend the most time on, and whether those sites are 'Very productive' or 'Very distracting'. It even gives you an overall productivity score.

If you're prone to wasting time on the internet, you need a browser add-on like this. It will amaze/horrify you how you spend your time.

Desktop and mobile versions that run in the background are also available. They break down how you spend your screen time, allowing you to work out how you spend it and how you could better organise it.

StayFocusd

StayFocusd is a Chrome add-on that allows you to limit how much time you spend on 'time-wasting' websites. You pick the sites you waste the most time on, then decide how much time you're allowed on them each day. Once you've used up that time, the site is blocked for the rest of the day. You can set them to only be accessible during certain times (like lunchtime) if you prefer. There are obvious ways around this, but if you're compelled to cheat you need to ask yourself how much you actually want to achieve your goals.

If you really struggle to avoid distractions, you can go 'nuclear' and block *everything* but your allowed sites (for instance, Novlr or ZenPen).

Similar browser add-ons include Self Control, Cold Turkey, LeechBlock, and Freedom.

Noisli

If you need to listen to background noise but find music too distracting, Noisli is for you. As well as a browser add-on for Chrome, there's also a browser-based version, and iOS and Android apps.

Noisli's tutorial of the browser-based version walks you through its features, and its sounds including rain, nature, coffee shops, and white noise. The interface is clean and simple, although the background colour changes when you have the browser version open, which I found distracting.

The browser version also has a distraction-free text editor, but it's quite basic compared to the other writing programs discussed earlier. That's not always a bad thing, though.

The browser add-on is free, but they have a paid-for app that you can download for your mobile device.

READ ALL ABOUT IT

Books

If writing is the exercise, then reading is the protein that builds the muscle. The more words written by other writers that you can soak up and learn from, the better your writing will be.

The books mentioned in this section have all inspired me in some way during the last few years. They look at mindset, time management, and creativity in ways I hadn't considered in the past. There's also some books on poetry, punctuation, and PR to get you started.

While I learned many things from these books, I don't agree with everything they say. Nevertheless, they're still worth a read – even if you don't agree with everything (or anything), you'll still learn a few new things. Something you disagree with may even inspire you to write a counterargument for a future piece of your own.

The Cambridge Companion to Creative Writing - David Morley

This was the first book I read for my MA. It's filled with advice for fiction writers, creative nonfiction writers, poets, and screenwriters. There are exercises for every form of writing in there, which is useful if you're looking to experiment and don't know where to start.

Unlike many textbooks, it's written in a fun, interesting way. Because of this, it's easy to dip in and out of and is a useful reference guide for many aspects of writing.

52 Ways of Looking at a Poem - Ruth Padel

Whether you've been writing poetry for years or you're just getting started, it's always interesting to see how someone else interprets a poem. There is no right or wrong answer when it comes to interpreting poetry, but seeing what someone else thinks helps you to see different points of view and can be a useful tool if you're just starting out.

This book contains all sorts of poems, then includes commentaries on each. I'd recommend reading the poems and annotating them yourself before you read the commentaries as you may pick up on different things. The more you learn to read between the lines of poetry, the more confident you'll become reading it, and the more you'll want to experiment with language.

My Grammar and I (Or Should That Be Me?): Old-School Ways to Sharpen Your English - Caroline Taggart and J.A. Wines

This is my favourite book on grammar. It makes some of the more complex grammatical concepts easier to understand and has tips that can benefit even the strictest grammar nerd. It's a fun read but it's also easy to dip in and out of for quick refreshers.

Eats, Shoots and Leaves - Lynne Truss

This is a classic book on grammar and should be a must-read for every writer. Both of my university courses had it at the top of their reading lists, and for good reason. *Eats, Shoots and Leaves* digs deep into the importance of good grammar. While some of the references are a little outdated now, the message still stands: punctuation is important!

Your Press Release is Breaking My Heart - Janet Murray

Janet Murray is a PR specialist with over 15 years experience working as a journalist. In *Your Press Release is Breaking my Heart*, she writes about why press releases aren't important anymore and how to get coverage in magazines, newspapers, and blogs. If you have issues with pitching of any kind, this is a must-read. She's also got an active and helpful Facebook community.

On Writing - Stephen King

Part memoir, part writing guide, Stephen King's *On Writing* is a must-read for every writer. He talks you through his writing process, the tools every writer needs, and gives an insight into the life of one of the world's most well-known writers.

One thing I don't particularly like is how he actively tries to discourage you from plotting. He is one of the lucky few that gets to write for a living. It's a whole lot easier for him to sit down with no idea where his book is going than it is for someone who also has a full-time job and a family to manage. Ultimately, it's a personal choice, but plotting makes completing a project a whole lot easier.

Save the Cat! The Last Book on Screenwriting That You'll Ever Need - Blake Snyder

Save the Cat is the book for you if you want to work on your plotting skills and don't know where to start. It's brutally honest about the state of the market and why most successful stories follow the same structure regardless of their genre. What works for screenwriting doesn't always work for fiction, but when it comes to the structure of a good story, there's little difference, so novelists will also find this book useful.

Big Magic - Elizabeth Gilbert

I disagree with the overall message of this book – that creativity is a form of 'big magic' – but I do think there are important lessons that can be taken away from it all the same.

Big Magic doesn't advise us to be fearless – instead, it advises us to be brave. Brave enough to share our creativity with the world, and brave enough to not let our fears hold us back. It's an inspiring read from someone who's battled anxiety all her life.

Feel the Fear and Do it Anyway - Susan Jeffers

Feel the Fear and Do it Anyway is one of the best-selling self-help books ever, and for good reason. If you feel like anxiety takes control of your life more than you'd like, and it's one of the reasons you haven't put your writing out there yet, you *need* to read this book. It looks into the causes of our fears and how the people in our lives can reinforce them without even realising it. The book also offers ways to overcome your fears and mantras to repeat to yourself when you're feeling anxious.

Quiet: The Power of Introverts in a World That Can't Stop Talking - Susan Cain

In a world that's obsessed with how big people's personalities are, being an introvert can often feel like a bad thing. *Quiet* thinks the opposite.

Quiet believes that even in the culture of personality, introversion is a positive trait that can be effectively used in all sorts of industries. Introverts have a different set of skills and priorities to extroverts, and by embracing them we bring something new to the table and stand out in our own way.

The Confidence Code - Katty Kay and Claire Shipman

While *The Confidence Code* is aimed at women, the studies and tips in it can benefit everyone. *The Confidence Code* looks at what motivates us and how confidence is about so much more than what you're born with – in fact, a lot of it is environmental. Some of the results from their experiments and interviews are surprising, and even surprised to the authors.

Until I read this book, it had never occurred to me that the opposite of confidence was anxiety. It sounds so obvious now, but at the time, I was battling my anxiety while insisting I was confident as a writer. I really, really wasn't.

If you're interesting in improving your confidence and lessening your anxiety, this book is a *must* read.

Black Box Thinking - Matthew Syed

As I've already mentioned, this is one of my favourite books. When I first started reading it, I had no idea how much it would affect me. While I wouldn't suggest reading it if you're in hospital or about to go on an aeroplane, I would advise reading it as soon as you can. It examines how we approach failure and how those that are the most successful see failure as a way to learn and grow, rather than a wall that stops them from progressing.

The book features interviews with doctors and pilots, as well as the likes of James Dyson and David Beckham. Said interviews prove that their successes weren't just down to talent: it was down to mindset, too.

By not shutting yourself off from failure you can be a

better person, and of course, a better writer.

Blogs

The great thing about blogs is that they offer free advice that's accessible to everyone. The worst thing about blogs is that they're free to create and accessible to everyone. This means that you can end up in a sea of information you don't want while unable to find the information you really need.

The blogs mentioned in this section have all been around for several years and are therefore treasure troves of information. Just because the information is offered for free, that doesn't mean that there wasn't still a huge amount of work put into each post.

If you're looking for inspiration to start your own blog, or you want to do some more research into a particular area, these blogs are good places to start.

Many of these blogs also have mailing lists that will send you monthly or weekly roundups, or even new posts straight to your inbox.

Buffer

https://blog.bufferapp.com/

Best for: Productivity, marketing, happiness, business.

The Buffer blog is my favourite. They're incredibly open about how they operate as a business, and regularly conduct marketing experiments and share their results. Their blog is divided into four sections: Open (productivity and work culture), Social (social media and online marketing), Overflow (development), and Happiness.

Their blog is where I first began to learn about online marketing, and it's part of why I have a job as a content marketer today. Their posts are long but easy-to-read, and when new social media features role out, they're one of the first to write about it.

Open, meanwhile, is filled with posts that will inspire your writing, marketing, and even your day job.

Copy Hackers

https://copyhackers.com/

Best for: Copywriting, marketing.

Copy Hackers is filled with in-depth advice to help you write better copy and boost your conversion rates. It gives you an estimated reading time for blog posts and many are half an hour to an hour. *That's* how in-depth we're talking.

Copy Hackers also offers free and paid-for courses on different elements of copywriting.

Copyblogger

http://www.copyblogger.com/blog/

Best for: Copywriting, marketing, mindset.

Copyblogger has been around since 2006, and has grown to become the go-to place for all things copywriting. Not only are there new posts most weekdays, but they also have a podcast, online course, and online community. Some of these are free to use, while others involve a fee.

If you want get started copywriting, their site will have the answers that you're looking for.

The Writer's Cookbook

https://www.writerscookbook.com/

Best for: Productivity, mindset, mental health.

Over at The Writer's Cookbook you'll find advice on writing, productivity, mental health, and self-publishing, as well as guest posts on traditional publishing. There's advice on how to write about particular topics such as anxiety or grief, as well as reviews of writing tools such as Novlr and Scrivener.

The Creative Penn

https://www.thecreativepenn.com/

Best for: Business, marketing, publishing, writing.

Joanna Penn was one of The Guardian's Top 100 creative professionals of 2013. Her blog, established in 2009, is filled with information and advice on writing and publishing that can help you whatever stage of your writing career you're at.

She also hosts a podcast of the same name, interviewing top businesspeople and authors on different topics each week. Transcripts of podcast episodes can be found on the blog.

Goins Writer

http://www.goinswriter.com/

Best for: Mindset, business, marketing.

Jeff Goins started off by committing to writing everyday. He's now published five books and his Tribe Writers course helps other writers to find audiences for their writing, too. Having struggled with his own inner demons that told him he shouldn't write, he often writes about mindset and motivation and how to overcome the self-doubt that tells you that you're not good enough. His writing style is a little tough-love at times, but this isn't a bad thing. He is brutally honest in his advice, and I like that about him.

Cathy's Comps and Calls

http://compsandcalls.com/

Best for: Writing prompts, competitions, submissions. Cathy Bryant has won over 25 literary awards and writing competitions and has been the judge for several. This makes her the perfection person to run a site about writing competitions and submission calls. Everything listed on her site is free to enter. Some submissions and competitions pay, some offer contributor copies, and others are just for fun. The site doesn't discriminate against what it features: if you can submit to it, Comps and Calls will cover it. The site is updated on the first of each month with a new list of submissions.

OVER TO YOU

To improve your writing and get through your mental blocks you need to channel as much of your creative energy as possible into writing. You need to learn to trust yourself, and that sense of trust only comes from perseverance. There is no easy way around it. The easy way is to stick with the status quo and never finish that project you started five years ago. Writing is hard. I don't blame you if you've changed your mind after reading this. But if you haven't, remember that you can and will get there. If you put the effort in. You will have to make sacrifices, but if you want to reach your end goal badly enough, you'll do whatever it takes.

There isn't a once-size-fits-all hack to being more productive or more comfortable in your writerly skin. What works for me may not work for you, but even if you don't follow the advice and tips in this book, I hope you enjoyed the journey we've been on, and it inspires you to write more, be kind to yourself, and make the most of the time that you have.

Being productive is all about developing enough self-awareness to know when you can work, when you can push yourself, and when you need to rest. Like all skills, it takes time to develop. We all have natural aptitudes towards some things over others, but I'm a firm believer that if our mind is open enough, we can learn anything. Great writing comes from the willingness to put the work in, and to accept that what you create will never be perfect. It's about trusting yourself during that journey and knowing that you can't always think like a creative – quite often, the 'fail fast' mantra of the programming world is far more beneficial than waiting for creativity to strike, as many writers do.

If you wait for inspiration, it may never come. It's not a bus, or a tram, or any other form of public transport. If you wait for long enough a bus will eventually show up, even if it's not the right one. Writing ability and creativity don't work like that. Writing and creativity are more like learning to drive – you need to take the time to learn the theory, then put that theory into practice. The more you drive, the better the driver you'll become.

However, even as you continue to learn it's still possible to fall into bad habits. Just the same as passengers can comment on bad driving habits, readers and editors can comment on bad writing habits. Taking onboard such comments pushes you closer towards your writing goal, whether that's to win a literary award, have legions of fans, make it onto a bestseller list, or be lucky enough to make a living from your craft. You won't get to join the members of those small, fortunate groups if you spend all day sat on the sofa, wishing you had more time, though. The people in those small, fortunate groups deserve their successes because they work their asses off. They took the time to work on their craft and had the gumption to think that it was good enough to share with the rest of the world.

Writing is a marathon. It takes time, patience, and hard work. It's a scary process. If you compare the 50,000+ words of a novel to the 26 miles and 385 yards of a marathon, just the thought of it is terrifying. But if you break those words down, it's less scary. It's attainable.

I know you can do it.

I know you *want* to do it.

That's why you bought this book.

So now go write.

You're out of excuses not to.

What's Stopping You?

1 Justine Tal Goldberg. *200 Million Americans Want to Publish Books, But Can They?* Publishing Perspectives. https://publishingperspectives.com/2011/05/200-million-americans-want-to-publish-books/

2 *New Study: 55% of YA books bought by adults.* Publishers Weekly. https://www.publishersweekly.com/pw/by-topic/childrens/childrens-industry-news/article/53937-new-study-55-of-ya-books-bought-by-adults.html

3 Aimee Groth. *You're The Average of the Five People You Spend the Most Time With.* Business Insider. http://www.businessinsider.com/jim-rohn-youre-the-average-of-the-five-people-you-spend-the-most-time-with-2012-7?IR=T

4 Angela K. Troyer Ph.D., C. Psych. *The Health Benefits of Socializing.* Psychology Today. https://www.psychologytoday.com/blog/living-mild-cognitive-impairment/201606/the-health-benefits-socializing

5 *The Great British Bake Off* Rules of Entry. https://love.take-part.co.uk/gbbo/info/rules

6 Alison Wood Brooks. *Get Excited: Reappraising Pre-Performance Anxiety as Excitement.* http://www2.apa.org/pubs/journals/releases/xge-a0035325.pdf

7 Daniel Ameduri. *7 Scientific Reasons Hugging is the Best Thing Ever.* Thought Catalog. https://thoughtcatalog.com/daniel-ameduri/2015/04/7-beneficial-effects-of-hugging-that-prove-you-should-do-it-more-often/

8 Heather Hatfield. *Power Down for Better Sleep.* WebMD. http://www.webmd.com/sleep-disorders/features/power-down-better-sleep

9 Christopher Bergland. *Exposure to Natural Light Improves Workplace Performance.* Psychology Today. https://www.psychologytoday.com/blog/the-athletes-way/201306/exposure-natural-light-improves-workplace-performance

Why Do You Write?

1 Richard Lea. *Most UK Authors' Annual Incomes Still Well Below Minimum Wage, Says Survey.* The Guardian. https://www.theguardian.com/books/2016/oct/19/uk-authors-annual-incomes-below-minimum-wage-survey-average-earnings

2 Stephen King, *On Writing* (London, Hodder & Stoughton, 2010)

3 J.K.Rowling. Tweet from 2016. https://twitter.com/jk_rowling/status/713298761288708096/

How Much Time Do You REALLY Have?

1 Loulla-Mae Elefheriou-Smith. *Community Buy Texas Man Car After Finding Him Walking 3 Miles to and From Work in 32 Degree Heat.* The Independent. https://www.independent.co.uk/news/world/americas/man-walk-to-from-work-home-heat-32-degree-buy-car-texas-community-justin-korva-andy-mitchell-a7813181.html

2 Carolyn Steber. *7 Benefits of a Solid Daily Routine.* Bustle. https://www.bustle.com/articles/148246-7-benefits-of-a-solid-daily-routine

3 Oliver Burkeman. *This Column Will Change Your Life: How Long Does it Really Take to Change a Habit?* The Guardian. https://www.theguardian.com/lifeandstyle/2009/oct/10/change-your-life-habit-28-day-rule

4 Eisenhower. http://www.eisenhower.me/eisenhower-matrix/

5 Heidi Grant Halvorson. *The Amazing Power of 'I Don't vs. 'I Can't'.* Forbes. https://www.forbes.com/sites/heidigranthalvorson/2013/03/14/the-amazing-power-of-i-dont-vs-i-cant/#30128100d037

6 Earl Miller. *Here's Why You Shouldn't Multitask, According to an MIT Neuroscientist.* Fortune. http://fortune.com/2016/12/07/why-you-shouldnt-multitask/

7 Gregory Ciotto. *How Music Affects Your Productivity*. Fast Company. https://www.fastcompany.com/3032868/how-music-affects-your-productivity

8 Damien Gayle. *Daily Commute of Two Hours – Reality for 3.7m UK Workers.* The Guardian. https://www.theguardian.com/money/2016/nov/18/daily-commute-of-two-hours-reality-for-37m-uk-workers

9 The Pomodoro Technique. Cirillo Company. https://cirillocompany.de/pages/pomodoro-technique

10 Allison Abrams, LCSW-R. *Mental Health and the Effects of Social Media*. Psychology Today. https://www.psychologytoday.com/blog/nurturing-self-compassion/201703/mental-health-and-the-effects-social-media

11 Gus Lubin and Rachel Gillett. *21 Successful People Who Wake up Incredibly Early.* Business Insider. http://uk.businessinsider.com/successful-people-who-wake-up-really-early-2016-4/

Making the Most of Every Minute

1 Bullet Journal - The Analog System for the Digital Age. http://bulletjournal.com/

2 Blake Snyder, *Save the Cat! The Last Book on Screenwriting You'll Ever Need.* (Los Angeles, Michael Wiese Productions, 2005)

3 *Rowling to Kill Two in Final Book.* BBC. http://news.bbc.co.uk/1/hi/entertainment/5119836.stm

4 Kevin McSpadden. *You Now Have a Shorter Attention Span Than a Goldfish.* Time. http://time.com/3858309/attention-spans-goldfish/

5 Eben Harrell. *How 1% Improvements Led to Olympic Gold.* https://hbr.org/2015/10/how-1-performance-improvements-led-to-olympic-gold

6 Matthew Syed. *Black Box Thinking.* (London, John Murray, 2016)

7 Lauren Marchese. *The Psychology of Checklists: Why Setting Small Goals Motivates Us to Accomplish Bigger Things.* Trello. https://blog.trello.com/the-psychology-of-checklists-why-setting-small-goals-motivates-us-to-accomplish-bigger-things

8 *Speeches: For The Average Person Speaking at a Normal Pace, What is the Typical Number of Words They Can Say in One Minute?* Quora. https://www.quora.com/Speeches-For-the-average-person-speaking-at-a-normal-pace-what-is-the-typical-number-of-words-they-can-say-in-one-minute

9 Joanna Penn. *23 Million Books Sold. How to Have a Successful Long Term Writing Career with Kevin J. Anderson.* The Creative Penn. https://www.thecreativepenn.com/2016/10/17/23-million-books-kevin-j-anderson/

10 *Patrick Kinna: Churchill's Wartime Secretary.* The Independent. https://www.independent.co.uk/news/obituaries/patrick-kinna-churchills-wartime-secretary-1707861.html

11 Jessica Gross. *Walking Meetings? 5 Surprising Thinkers Who Swore by*

Them. Ted Talks. http://blog.ted.com/walking-meetings-5-surprising-thinkers-who-swore-by-them/

How to Write More

1 Philip Moeller. *Why Learning Leads to Happiness.* The Huffington Post. http://www.huffingtonpost.com/2012/04/10/learning-happiness_n_1415568.html

2 Bill Gates. Gates Notes. https://www.gatesnotes.com/Books

3 *JKRowling: Hermione Should've Married Harry, Not Ron.* The Guardian. https://www.theguardian.com/books/2014/feb/02/jk-rowling-hermione-harry-ron-married

4 Justin Bariso. *20 Years Ago, Steve Jobs Demonstrated the Perfect Way to Respond to an Insult.* Inc. https://www.inc.com/justin-bariso/20-years-ago-steve-jobs-demonstrated-the-perfect-w.html

5 Gina Trapani. *Jerry Seinfeld's Productivity Secret.* Life Hacker. https://lifehacker.com/281626/jerry-seinfelds-productivity-secret

6 *How Much Sleep Do We Need?* Loyola University Chicago Stritch School of Medicine. https://www.eurekalert.org/pub_releases/2015-02/luhs-hms021115.php

7 *Get a Jolt with the 'Caffeine Nap'.* World Lifestyle. http://www.worldlifestyle.com/health/get-jolt-caffeine-nap

8 *Stages of Sleep and Sleep Cycles.* Tuck. https://www.tuck.com/stages/#what_is_a_sleep_cycle_

Made in the USA
Middletown, DE
18 March 2018